THE BOOK OF SURRENDER

Other New Age Titles from Prentice Hall Press

by Jane Roberts
Dreams, "Evolution," and Value Fulfillment, Volume I
Dreams, "Evolution," and Value Fulfillment, Volume II
The Individual and the Nature of Mass Events
The Nature of Personal Reality
The Nature of the Psyche
The Seth Material
Seth Speaks
The "Unknown" Reality, Volume 1
The "Unknown" Reality, Volume 2
The Afterdeath Journal of an American Philosopher
The God of Jane
Psychic Politics
The Education of Oversoul Seven
Oversoul Seven and the Museum of Time

by Nancy Ashley
Create Your Own Reality: A Seth Workbook

by Susan M. Watkins
Conversations with Seth, Volume I
Conversations with Seth, Volume II

THE
BOOK OF
SURRENDER

A Journey to Self-Awareness
Inspired by the Words of Emmanuel

Wingate Paine

PRENTICE
HALL
PRESS

New York London Toronto Sydney Tokyo Singapore

The Book of Surrender was written by Wingate Paine, who spoke to the being of golden light known as Emmanuel through Emmanuel's channel, Pat Rodegast. *The Book of Surrender* is neither a sequel nor a companion to Pat Rodegast's work, *Emmanuel's Book*, and neither Pat Rodegast nor any of the authors or writers associated with *Emmanuel's Book* are in any way associated with the publication of *The Book of Surrender*.

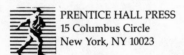 PRENTICE HALL PRESS
15 Columbus Circle
New York, NY 10023

Copyright © 1987 by Communion of Souls Foundation

PRENTICE HALL PRESS and colophons are registered trademarks of Simon & Schuster, Inc.

Library of Congress Cataloging-in-Publication Data

Paine, Wingate.
   The book of surrender.

   1. Spiritual life.   2. Paine, Wingate.   3. Emmanuel (Spirit)   I. Emmanuel (Spirit)   II. Title.
BL624.P25   1987   133.9'3   87-42673
ISBN 0-13-086687-3

Designed by C. Linda Dingler

Manufactured in the United States of America

10   9   8   7   6   5   4   3   2

Contents

CONTENTS

< vi >

Foreword

This is the story of an unusual man named Wingate. A Mayflower New Englander, a graduate of Andover and Yale, with a long family tradition in banking, ministry, and the law, he gave up a promising career in business and at the age of thirty became a photographer. Only six months after buying his first camera, he began his rapid rise to the height of his profession, where he remained for twenty years. He was a perennial winner of top international awards, and a book of his photographs became a contemporary classic.

He lived with his beautiful wife and two children on Fifth Avenue in an apartment that on certain occasions had all three fireplaces going, and summered at a hideaway on a lake in Connecticut. He drove a red 1970 Jaguar XJ and had a Lincoln Continental Mark IV for formal affairs. He kept a box at the Met, another at Carnegie Hall. His suits were impeccably tailored, and he had a private cellar of vintage wines. He was known to spend a long weekend at the Ritz in Paris or Claridge's in London, and on special evenings a string

< vii >

quartet from the American Symphony would play Mozart in his living room.

And then, almost overnight, he gave up everything he had built his success on.

I first met Wingate in the spring of 1972. The andromeda bushes and weeping birch trees in his widely acclaimed roof garden were in bloom, and Tibetan bells chimed softly throughout his studio. I was terrified of him. There were still traces of his nickname, "Tyrannosaurus Rex," in his furrowed brow and the firmness of his full lips. His penetrating blue eyes took me in with the speed of a camera shutter.

And yet there was a vulnerability to him. A sense of confusion, I thought, playing beneath his stern exterior. He had been one of those powerful men who could marshal their talent to mold life on a grand scale; but then, once he achieved his dreams, he realized they hadn't brought him what he thought he was seeking.

So it wasn't really a confusion I detected in him. It was a gentle inner light struggling to shine through the density of the enormously successful life he had created. In the same way that he had assembled the machinery to succeed, he was now beginning the arduous process of dismantling it step by step to find another kind of life for himself. At a time when most people his age and in his position were moving to Palm Beach or taking cruises around the world, he was embarking on a pilgrim's progress to higher truth.

He had been studying meditation for several years and teaching classes in growing consciousness when I was introduced to him by a mutual friend. He invited me to attend his class, and I soon began practicing meditation with him and his group. Gradually a friend-

< viii >

ship developed. In time, he would found the Growth Center, a kind of school for inner transformation, and we worked together putting out a newsletter on human awareness.

During the early years of our relationship, I watched him undergo a number of major life changes, some self-imposed, others not. He would get divorced, leave his Fifth Avenue apartment, sell his Connecticut home, his cars, his wine. Eventually he moved into an ashram. He had made the commitment to transform himself, and while this certainly wasn't the only path to self-discovery he could have chosen, he wanted to live in an environment in which the changes could occur to their fullest possible extent. The austere life, however, was not entirely new to him. During World War II, when he could have been exempt from service because he was nearly blind in one eye, he left his family and home to join the Marines, and eventually he rose in rank from boot to captain.

But now he had a new war, an inner war. He was again ready to serve. His room at the ashram was nothing more than a cell, simply decorated with a purple carpet, a chair, a small chest, and a captain's bed. He had come to discover who he really was and what his new purpose in life might be.

At the time, I didn't understand that what I felt was an extreme withdrawal, and I drifted away from him. Five years passed before we would again have contact. I had heard that he moved out of the ashram and was now an initiated teacher and an ordained minister. I visited with him and soon again started sitting with his group.

A few remnants of his old life had been moved into

< ix >

his Center: a cushioned chair, a marble table, a painting. He seemed settled within himself, happier, more assured of his direction as man and spiritual teacher. Yet, in spite of his new sense of self, I felt he was still in search of something. Though the inner light had cracked the surface, softening him, making him more charitable and compassionate, he was still groping for answers, or perhaps a Teacher who would bring him greater knowledge.

That opportunity presented itself in the autumn of 1977. He had been invited to go to Westport, Connecticut, to meet with the channel for a spiritual being named Emmanuel. He went out of curiosity and ostensibly for only one session. To his amazement, he found in this being from "the other side" a kind friend and his next Teacher and felt drawn to return to communicate with him again and again, doing so for six years.

In January 1983, I resumed my professional relationship with Wingate, helping him prepare for publication *Tilling the Soul*, a book on contemporary spiritual wisdom and practices that he had been working on for ten years. During this time, he passed on to me several tapes of the dialogues he had had with Emmanuel, to suggest quotes for inclusion in *Tilling the Soul*. I was immediately struck by the quality of these exchanges. In a very natural way, they told the story of a Seeker encountering his Teacher and the Teacher guiding the Seeker step by step to the ultimate lesson, the surrender to God's Will.

It was a remarkable story, this man's transformation through immense spiritual and physical challenges, including his struggle with cancer, which he overcame with Emmanuel's constant encouragement. It was made

< x >

even more unusual and startling because I was asked to believe that the extraordinary guidance was coming from a supposed disembodied being, and I usually don't put much credence in spirits from beyond. Yet as I read and reread the transcripts, I found myself more and more attracted to the spirit named Emmanuel. His warm, gentlemanly manner, which at times was marvelously humorous as well as quaint, like that of a poet from another age, made me feel that I was in the presence of a real friend. But it was principally his words, which I found myself increasingly returning to, out of both professional and personal interest, that always nourished me and made me feel renewed.

One of the most enigmatic aspects of this collection of twenty-two dialogues, which I still haven't comfortably resolved for myself, is the continuity of Emmanuel's interaction with Wingate from session to session, as if no time had elapsed in between. This in itself is astonishing, for his channel saw as many as six people a day five days a week, which means that thousands of other people communicated with Emmanuel during the six years.

I can't recall how the idea for *The Book of Surrender* originated, or where the title came from. I do remember that when I initially approached Wingate with the suggestion of making a book out of the dialogues, he was greatly reluctant. A private man, he felt the material was too personal. Yet he knew better than I the richness of Emmanuel's teachings and, believing that they would serve others as well, eventually agreed with my suggestion.

And while this is the story of one man's evolution from pilgrim to Teacher and Healer, ordinary man to

< xi >

Man of God, it is also everyone's—the story of all who have ever wondered who they really were and what they could truly be, and who dared to take the steps to answer for themselves these monumental questions.

—ALLAN RICHARDS

< xii >

THE BOOK OF SURRENDER

DIALOGUE ONE

28 October 1977

On a bright and sunny October morning, Wingate drove up the tree-lined Merritt Parkway to a house on a quiet street in the town of Westport, Connecticut.

He was greeted at the door by a vibrant, earthy woman and taken to a small but attractive room, simply furnished with two chairs facing each other, a low table with a tape recorder, and a large plant in one corner, where he would spend the next hour in what he anticipated would be the usual psychic reading.

E: Good morning, my friend. It is most pleasant to be with you again. That surprises you, does it not, but we have known each other in previous lives, and this meeting today is the result of a commitment that we made a long time ago.

The path that you have followed in these past years has been circuitous and sometimes tremendously torturous, has it not, yet it has brought you very close to your desired and yearned-for goal of Cosmic Consciousness, which I see you attaining in this lifetime.

In your meditative state you are becoming aware most certainly of the Spirit figures who are with you and of their energizing effect upon you, and you are beginning to take advantage of their help, which has been available to you all along.

< 1 >

There is a question in your mind as to what path you should now take, whether it is one that bears the insignia of Physical Healer or that of a Teacher of Truth, or whether there is in the center of these two wholes a blending that is truly much more uniquely you.

The love that you have for humankind is quite beautiful, and in that the healing capacities are indeed open. And yet your desire to be a Physical Healer is not quite as strong as the other urging deep within you that tells you quite correctly that the physical is merely the outer manifestation of the Spiritual and that healing must therefore take place on many levels, and the words that come to you and that will come to you far more abundantly as you progress on your path will be the principal healing elements in your Ministry. However, the fact that things you will feel yourself compelled to say or write have within them a healing truth need not deny you the right to place your hands upon an ailing fellow human being when the urge is very strong.

You have come into this incarnation with a variety of extremely developed talents and a tremendous backlog of information which you are now able, in the name of Service and of your own Soul's progress, to blend to a single purpose, and this blending will enrich not only the purpose but the abilities as well. Indeed, you are reaching the point in your evolution of Consciousness where Pure Service is possible, and you therefore are approaching the termination of your reincarnational cycle. I assume that's good news for you.

W: Yes, yes. Is it all right, my speaking to you directly the way I just did?

< 2 >

E: Oh, most certainly, most certainly. There are no rules of protocol here. View me as One with you in the Universe and speak to me comfortably, for we are all inhabitants of the same Reality. There is no need to place this communication from you in a sense of wonder.

W: Then I would like to ask you how this Center that I have and that I have been putting so much energy into for the last few years fits in with all the wonderful things you've been talking about. It just doesn't seem to be going anywhere, and it's as though my heart is being broken.

E: The reason for your feeling that the energy flow is not kind to you is that you have unwittingly restricted your own energy output in the choosing of the areas that you will touch upon and those that you will not. The outer manifestations of one's life are always an indication unfailingly of the limitations that are being experienced within. You are experiencing caution and a reluctance to move into a broader expanse of functioning, and although there is a great comfort in feeling that your world is very much the size that you can handle, you are underestimating your importance by keeping yourself enclosed in such a small area.

Please understand that you are indeed of Divine aspect. You are on the path not only of your own realization but of assisting others in their realization as well, and with such Divine purpose it seems foolish to be concerned about the future of your Center. Simply rest as comfortably as you can in the wisdom of your Higher Self, of your Soul, and allow this aspect to direct

< 3 >

the workings of your physical reality. You do this through meditation, as you know, but when your meditation has been completed, you must leave the door open to your Higher Wisdom, so that the wisdom can be given to you twenty-four hours a day. As your faith is strengthened you will find that there is no longer the need to have a sense of control, that things will flow as they will, and that you will flow with them, to your great delight and benefit.

W: I can't help but be a little troubled and a little puzzled by your suggestion that I reach out to new areas of expansion. For one thing, I don't know what direction to take—that's the puzzled part—and the troubled part is that I feel that it's time for me to be alone a lot to find out what it is I really know, like Thoreau, who learned "by travelling extensively in Concord." That idea has always appealed to me, yet of course one can also learn by traveling all over the world, and perhaps I've overdone the Concord thing.

E: There is always and will always be a necessity to seek within yourself your own truths and realizations. That is the only place you will find them, as you wisely know. But your reluctance to reach out to unknown areas, or those that you have not chosen, is indicative of the fact that you feel that you will not be quite safe, and that smallness is indeed more comfortable because of the control it gives you. This is a fear you must challenge every step of the way through touching the inner Light, and through the perfect belief that you are indeed Divinely guided.

< 4 >

W: Recently I've found myself jotting down some of my truths and realizations, as well a some of the practices that I use, with the thought that someday they might become a kind of growth book that I have thought of calling *Tilling the Soul*, which those who come to study with me might find useful. I wonder if this might not also be a way for me to reach out to more people, as you are suggesting.

E: It most certainly will. Your writing—and this is not the last book you will write—will in the future, if you so choose it, take on tremendous proportions as a very important aspect of your Ministry. This in turn will bring to you people who are desirous of learning from you and from the inspirational wisdom that you project in your writing.

W: Do you see me continuing my teaching in New York, or will I be moving to some other part of the country?

E: Put aside the need to know some future design and simply leave your life open to what is needed of it by the Divine forces. Once one has committed oneself to a life of Service, then the next most intelligent and useful step is to let go of the reins of one's life and allow the Divine energies to place one where one needs to be.

My friend, you have committed yourself to a life of Service, you have crossed the threshold into that area where you wish to be a channel of Divine wisdom, and now you need to confront within you and to overcome the sense that you will not find yourself safe and that

< 5 >

perhaps nothing at all will happen, and simply let the energies come through you. You have elected to flow with the Divine energies, so how can you possibly know where you are needed? You can only follow the dictates of your ever-opening heart and trust that what your Intuition tells you will ultimately prove to be the most beneficial.

W: That's beautiful, but I feel that my own Intuition is pretty undeveloped, and so I wonder if you would mind being a kind of surrogate Intuition, at least for a while.

E: Your Intuition is more developed than you suppose. It is your Intuition that is the clear impulse, and it is your human intellect that grabs that impulse and de-energizes it.

W: This is all so new to me, and a little frustrating, because I'm never quite sure whether it's my Intuition or something else that's guiding me.

E: It is always difficult when one is just beginning to recognize the voice of one's Intuition to trust that voice, when for so many years there has been the voice of self-will, that self-sustaining, self-serving energy that in the past has answered all one's questions. When I speak of listening to Intuition, I speak of the responsibility that you have to clarify that Intuition and to free it from the controlling interests of your conscious mind. It is wise for you to question, of course, but ultimately Intuition will be your guide, as it has been your guide throughout your whole life,

< 6 >

although it has been done under the guise of many other aspects of your conscious mind.

W: You said in the beginning that I was becoming aware of the Spirit figures who are with me, and I really feel that I am, especially in my meditation, where I have a sense of there being six or seven of us sitting around in a circle. It's very fragile, very subtle still, and yet here I am already wondering if at a certain point the only way I'm going to become more conscious is by blending and merging my Consciousness with theirs and theirs with mine in a greater and more expanded Reality.

E: Exactly, but one reaches this level of awareness through communion with other Souls on the physical plane as well as the Spiritual Plane, much as one reaches God's Love through the love of other human beings, and so the need to interchange with the energies of other Souls on the physical plane is a most important aspect of the phase of Soul existence that you are now moving into.

Indeed, many highly evolved Souls are in manifestation at this time and are being called together and will come together in a realized Spiritual community, a community of Souls, if you will, which is already in existence. You and these Souls in physical bodies with whom you will associate and a few that you have already associated with are a part of that next step, that blending into a wider and more conscious Soul Family which will ultimately extend across all seeming barriers of sect or nationality in the true Brotherhood of Man.

W: And when do you feel I'll be ready for this exciting new step, Emmanuel?

< 7 >

E: Once you have identified to your satisfaction your concepts, your teachings, when you feel that you are able to present in a coherent way, in an organized way, the meaning of your life and what you have to offer— once that foundation has been established, then it will be time for you to blend your thoughts and your energies with others, even those who may have had diametrically opposed experiences in their Soul growth. Your uniqueness will never be lost, nor will theirs, but in the blending there will be a deeper understanding and a greater truth, and this turn will serve a great many more people.

< 8 >

DIALOGUE TWO

21 November 1977

E: It is indeed a pleasure to see you again after such a short interval of time.

W: I know it's been short, but I'm a very confused guy right now. For example, last time I was here you suggested that things needed to change at the Center, that it was keeping me from growing, that I must flow more with the energies that are being presented to me, that I must trust more, trust myself more, trust my Intuition more, and I'm just not sure how to go about doing all this.

E: My friend, there are many reasons for a Soul's choosing to reincarnate, all of them without exception being devoted to the process of the Soul's growth. And so when one is presented with what seems to be a rather difficult obstacle, one can be very sure that that obstacle is of utmost importance to the progress of the Soul, that obstacles are only lessons to be learned, awarenesses to become conscious of, and that the obstacles that you are experiencing at this time are

< 9 >

neither insurmountable nor unmovable, but very valuable denials within the conscious mind that are there to
focus your attention on the Spiritual truths within and
therefore bring them to light. And therefore the Soul
arranges for different facets of a life to become difficult
so that the Consciousness can be brought to bear upon
those particular areas and the circumstances altered.

The difficulty that you feel you are experiencing in
the letting go of your doubt and your humanness and
in accepting the divinity of yourself is most
understandable. It is most difficult to be born into a
physical, finite reality and be advised that it is infinite,
to touch fear within your heart and be told that there is
no need for fear, to feel confusion in your mind and be
told that all is clear and light. And yes, it is most
difficult to be told that you must free yourself from the
chains of your humanness, to trust your human
condition, to trust your inner wisdom and abilities, to
know that what seems most physical is most Divine,
and to accept this duality which is the very nature of
your physical world and allow it to become one holistic
entity within you.

It is only your conscious mind, your physical human
mind, that separates you from the Divine aspects of
your Being. And the way to open the door to your
Divine Intuition, if we may use that phrase to cover the
many aspects of your developing awareness of your
Divinity and your Oneness with God, is first to trust
that it is there, and then to trust that you are worthy of
experiencing it. And then again to trust that all those
who are human are worthy of experiencing their
Divine Intuition also. And then to know that the road
to that Divine Intuition is through self-love and

< 10 >

through the acceptance of the Universe as it is, of your life as it is, knowing that always and ever there is a guidance and a protection and that there is most assuredly a reason for every happening. And when this broad aspect of acceptance is incorporated into your conscious mind, into your conscious living, then you will find your progress to be very rapid indeed.

But there's confusion and concern about something else, my friend, is there not?

W: Yes, yes, there is, Emmanuel, and I guess that's the real reason why I'm here. Last summer during a routine physical examination I was told I had a suspicious growth on my prostate and was sent to a urologist, who suggested watching it through the summer and seeing what happened. Unhappily, it kept getting larger, and last week he urged me to have a biopsy and at the same time said he felt eighty percent sure it was malignant.

E: It most certainly is.

W: Ouch. I was afraid you were going to say that.

E: And there is a need to remove the growth. Such an operation will be successful, and it would be wise for you to move in that direction as quickly as possible.

W: All the doctor is talking about is a simple exploratory operation, a biopsy.

E: I know, but I'm suggesting surgical removal of the problem.

< 11 >

W: I have such resistance to surgery, especially there. I feel that a better path for me rather than the traditional one is to go with things like detoxifying and regenerating my body through working with healing energies and visualization and affirmation and things like that.

E: Your innate distrust of surgical procedures must undergo certain alterations. The surgical field was begun by Divine Intervention, and there is no need to hold in question those who are lighted and who are caring, healing people. There are many in the medical profession who are proficient in their craft, and that doctor to whom you spoke is an honest man and is not prone to exaggeration. I assure you that you will be quite all right and the operation I am suggesting will be successful.

Though your Soul is confronting an unpleasant situation, and though there are various ways to sidestep the surgical procedure and work with alternate healing practices, I want to suggest to you that there is a need for an openness of mind and of heart. Your denial of the benefits of surgery are part and parcel of a blanket condemnation of the medical profession which is quite understandable, but there are those who are excellent in their art, and though the choice is yours, my friend, it is wise to challenge your fear.

But no chemotherapy. No radiation. They have failed many times in the treatment of malignancy, and in their failure have brought down the life of the patient being treated. And while I can assure you that it is necessary for those who die of radiation and chemotherapy to experience just such a thing, they are not wise for you.

< 12 >

W: Then you are suggesting that I go with surgery rather than the nontraditional alternatives that I mentioned.

E: Indeed I am. I am suggesting that the most direct and painless route is surgery. However, I do urge that if you choose to test the others, then do so by all means, for you must listen to your inner voice and your heart must be satisfied. But give yourself a reasonable amount of time in which to achieve results, and then if your approach doesn't seem to be working, be courageous enough to move into the more practiced method of surgical removal.

W: What you seem to be saying is that my approach is not going to work.

E: No, not at all. I'm simply saying that if it does not work, give yourself the time to go back to surgery.

W: Can we go over this one more time, because it's very important to me and I'm a little confused. It seems that what you're saying is that I am going to have the operation and that it will be successful. Meanwhile, if I feel the need to explore other things, go ahead and do it, because I must be satisfied that they're not going to work before I will feel right about going into surgery. So go ahead and try them, give yourself a reasonable amount of time to see that they're not going to work, and then go ahead and have the surgery done.

E: I'm only suggesting the most direct route. I do not say that the others will not work, but there is a need for

< 13 >

you to overcome your unreasoning dread of surgery. This is an important lesson for you.

W: It is. I know it is. As a matter of fact, as soon as I was told by this doctor that I would require surgery if the growth on my prostate turned out to be malignant, I started working on my resistance to it and really felt that I had worked through it. It was the Plan, it was what my Soul needed to experience, and yet I was going to do everything I could to avoid it because that was part of what my Soul needed to experience also.

But when you said I was going to have an operation and it would be successful, I wasn't even listening to the "successful" part—all I heard was "operation." So I still have resistance to work through, but if I can succeed in working through my resistance to surgery, which seems to be the important thing, then perhaps I won't need the operation after all.

E: Exactly. The Soul works in strange and wonderful ways, and as the conscious mind accepts the wisdom of the Soul each experience becomes a Spiritual gift. My friend, you have accepted your physical malfunction as such and are blessed in your wisdom and your understanding, and this will bring you most assuredly to the other side of light and health in this life.

< 14 >

DIALOGUE THREE

3 December 1977

W: I've just been in contact with my urologist, who did a biopsy before Thanksgiving, and finally, finally the results have come back, and they show that my tumor is indeed malignant. Which of course was no big surprise—you had already said it was anyway. But then when I asked him how soon I should have surgery and he came right back with "Yesterday," I guess I panicked a little bit, and I can't tell you how grateful I am, Emmanuel, that you and your channel agreed to this unusual communication-by-telephone, which I'm sure is very difficult for you both, but I don't know what to do next and you have become my closest adviser and the one person I feel I can really trust.

E: My dear friend, let me assure you before we go one step further that the stress that has been laid upon haste is quite unnecessary.

W: That's such a relief, Emmanuel, such a relief; now I feel I have time to look around for another surgeon without taking a chance of having the cancer spread to

< 15 >

other parts of my body while I do it, and after that "Yesterday" remark I just don't want to have anything to do with the doctor I've been seeing. I've already made an appointment to see someone else who's been highly recommended to me, and I feel good about him just from having talked to him on the telephone.

E: I encourage you to trust your feelings in this matter.

W: But what about the timing? Do you have any suggestions as to when you think the surgery should take place?

E: Again, the stress laid upon haste is quite unnecessary. There is no need here for deep concern. The problem will be corrected, and I suggest that you have it taken care of at your convenience.

W: This new doctor will be away until early January, and so that's the earliest it could be done.

E: In the interim would be an ideal time to experiment with the many areas of alternate healing that your active mind has carried you into.

W: With the thought of succeeding, Emmanuel, or just with the thought of experimenting.

E: With the thought of success, of course, or at least of alleviating the problem. There isn't enough time for complete success.

W: I've already changed my diet pretty dramatically, and I've started working with healing energy and using

< 16 >

visualization and affirmation, and this feels very good to me.

E: There is no question but that this is an effective approach.

W: I'm also beginning to see my cancer as something that the Soul-me planned to have happen because the Wingate-me needed it for his growth.

E: Absolutely, there is no question about it.

W: And I'm learning to accept it more and more, not quite joyously yet, but still to accept it and look for the good in it.

E: There is great beauty here in the deep faith that you are developing. Indeed, it has grown in strength until it has become the mainstay of your existence. What more could you ask? With a faith such as yours, what is there that you have to fear? Nothing. My dear friend, all is well.

< 17 >

DIALOGUE FOUR

27 December 1977

W: Emmanuel, is it all right if we begin with me talking a little about what I've been up to since I saw you last?

E: Of course, my friend, most certainly.

W: Well, to begin with, I made a date for surgery with the doctor I told you I was going to see, but the more I thought about it the more I found myself resisting it, and yesterday I wrote him a letter saying that something had come up and I had to cancel it. And I don't think I did it because I am afraid of surgery. I don't like the idea, but I'm not a coward. I think I did it because I discovered that the operation involved implanting radioactive rods in my prostate and the thought of radiation really bothered me. And then I discovered that this practice used to be done on the West Coast while complete removal of the prostate was the standard practice on the East Coast and now it's just the other way around, and that bothered me also. I couldn't help but wonder if either one of them was all that effective.

< 18 >

And then I found myself resisting the traditional approach to all disease and instead being drawn more and more to alternative methods like naturopathy, which goes about as far as you can go. It says that there is basically only one disease, there is only one cause, and there is only one cure, that in one way or another our bodies become toxic and that this toxicity then manifests itself wherever there is a weak spot, which in my case happened to be my prostate, and that the best way to deal with such a manifestation is to first get rid of the body's toxicity and then to give the body whatever it needs to regenerate itself.

It's as though the body, which is ninety percent water anyway, was a lake, much like the one where I used to spend my weekends and vacations. It was crystal clear when I first bought land and built there—you could easily see bottom in thirty feet of water—but then over the years as more and more people built around it and dumped their toxic wastes into it, and more and more motorboats leaked their gasoline and oil into it and planes spread their pesticides all over it, the water became murky with algae and the bottom that was so clear before began silting up and the oxygen level began going down, and finally strange plants that thrive in this kind of low-energy environment began growing in the coves.

I think of my prostate as being like one of those coves, and the cancer cells as being like those strange plants, which you could get rid of by pulling them out by the roots or by spraying them with a chemical that would kill them, or you could set fire to them and try to kill them that way. In other words, with surgery or chemotherapy or radiation. But there's always the chance you

< 19 >

wouldn't get them all, and in any case they would probably come up again or start growing somewhere else because you hadn't done anything to change the conditions that were favorable to their growth in the first place, except to make them even more favorable.

Or finally you could stop putting things into the lake and onto the lake that are toxic and poisonous and begin doing things that would help the lake to clean itself out and regenerate itself, and I've started on an intensive program with special emphasis on nutrition that is designed to do this. I've also been intensifying my work with the healing energies, first telling myself that the cancer cells are not bad cells to be destroyed but sick cells to be given love and caring and good food and fresh air that will help them get well again. And then I visualize a brilliant white light surrounding my prostate to keep it from spreading while I affirm that the malignant growth is getting smaller and smaller. And then finally I picture this light interpenetrating my prostate and filling every sick cell with its cleansing, healing, vitalizing energy.

E: My friend, there is a deep desire within me to commend you for your courage in choosing this path. The prospect of immediate healing is a siren song that is a lure to many, but unless the overall condition is taken care of, as you are now doing, the problem will reappear in other places in a very short time, and therefore your total approach is a very valid one and the nutritional program that you are on, if it is done in a controlled way, in a sensible way, not allowing the toxins to be

< 20 >

released too quickly, will be very valuable. Just be sure that you remain aware of the possibility of self-poisoning and be cautious of that.

W: That's always a danger, I know. But it also seems to be an unavoidable part of the healing process that I may just have to go through. But the thing I like about all this is that it feels positive and creative, while the other possibilities seem to me to be destructive and negative. And you know, Emmanuel, I feel the cancer is only the tip of the iceberg, which is warning me that I need to clean up my lake and keep it clean.

E: Indeed, this opportunity that your body has presented you with through the instigation of your Soul to test your faith, to walk with your faith and to realize its power, is a most important step in your evolutionary process. Listen to your heart in its desire to touch God in this matter, and to the voice of your inner wisdom that is directing you so faultlessly in your efforts.

My friend, your faith and your determination to walk the path that you have chosen are already manifesting in the alleviation of your problem. Indeed, the intense energy field that you have placed around the cancerous growth has blocked any future expansion, and your efforts to disintegrate the growth itself are beginning to take effect.

W: Would you just say that again, Emmanuel, that I'm getting better? That's the first encouragement I've had since the discovery of the growth last May, and I really needed to hear it because this program I'm on isn't all

< 21 >

that easy. My diet of eighty percent raw fruits and vegetables might be all right in the middle of July, but it just doesn't make it in the middle of December. Drinking a glass of cold carrot juice is not the same as having a bowl of hot black bean soup.

And it seems as though my whole life has become nothing but finding the right food, preparing and eating it, cleaning up afterward, taking endless supplements, seeing doctors. There's literally no time left for anything else. My teaching and writing have come to a screeching halt, and my social life, which used to revolve around mealtimes, is now practically nonexistent. And then there are those loving friends and relatives who would feel much better if I were in the hospital having surgery or chemotherapy or radiation treatment, and I don't blame them. Certainly no traditional doctor would advise me to do what I'm doing.

E: Let me express my understanding and concern for your position and my most hearty accolade for the direction that you have chosen to follow. We will walk this path together, my friend, and you will be victorious.

W: "We will walk this path together, my friend, and you will be victorious." I have a feeling I'm going to be repeating those words in the middle of many anxious nights this winter. When I'm strong I know that this is the right path for me. If I die, I die, but it's still something I must do anyway. But then there are times when I'm weak and the doubts and the fears creep in, like two or three weeks ago. There I was, lying in bed feeling pretty depressed and thinking about my cancer and how I didn't want to die, and this little voice said,

< 22 >

"You're going to, you know. Someday." And I said, "Well, I don't want to die yet then," and the voice said, "Why?" so I had to work with that a little bit, and then I found myself saying, "Because I don't want to move to Los Angeles."

Of course, it wasn't moving to Los Angeles that was the problem, it was my resistance to moving to any strange place. My friends are here, my work is here, all the places I'm familiar with are here. But now I know you, Emmanuel, and you're certainly a friend, and there's my Soul Family that I'm also beginning to feel closer to, and this makes it a lot easier for me to think about moving on.

E: But not yet, dear friend, not yet. You still have a lot of work to do in this lifetime, and in this connection I am beginning to speak to you directly at times and feel that you are aware of this.

W: But it's such a little awareness, Emmanuel. Isn't there some way or something I could do to help me become more aware?

E: Indeed there is. First be aware of my intent to communicate with you on a one-to-one basis, and then as you feel a desire to speak to me allow that desire to be the signal that I am near. To be sure, it is all a matter of trust. It begins to sound like an endless repetition, does it not, my friend, this business of it all being a matter of trusting, and yet no stronger Truth can be stated. Many say that trust can be an illusion, and that if one lives only on trust, one lives an illusion. This is nonsense. Illusion is when a Soul enters a life and feels

< 23 >

that there is no hope, that there is no God, that there is no reason to a Universe that seems cruelly chaotic. That is illusion, and I speak not of Illusion but of Truth.

W: Won't this program I'm on also help me to become more aware?

E: There is no question about it. When I speak of you and I am communicating directly, I am speaking not only to the reality of your developing abilities to hear more clearly but also to the lifting of the energies of your body and the heightening of your spirituality as a result of what you are doing. But let me be quick to assure you that in this direct communication it is not my intent to displace those Spirit Beings who have always been with you, and of course this cannot and should not and will not be done. You do know my voice, however, you do know my vibration, you do know me, and this will serve as a bridge, perhaps, that will help you in your communication, not only with me, but also with those other dear Souls who are with you. I do this out of love, and because of the deep Service that you are doing in this lifetime. There is much beauty within you, my friend, there is much productivity, much value to those fortunate enough to know you, to come in contact with you. Indeed, you are building an edifice that will continue indefinitely.

W: I'm not sure I understand what you mean by "edifice," Emmanuel.

E: I was referring to your life and all that emanates from it. In its very beginning a life can be likened to the

< 24 >

raw materials that a builder has in hand as he envisions a beautiful edifice, and the living of that life can be likened to the erection, to the putting together of that edifice. It is like alchemy, taking the clay of physicality and breathing Spirit into it and changing that clay into gold, which of course is what you are doing now with this illness, taking the physical and breathing Spirit into it.

W: Will I be able to help other people do that with their physical problems?

E: Perhaps, but what you have to offer goes much further than that, for you will be dealing not just with malfunctions of the body but with a total concept of Spiritual Truth manifested in physical reality. Indeed, you already know and are learning more and more that the physical life and the Spiritual Life do not need to be thought of as divided and separate, but that they are in reality one and the same, and this is a message that must be expressed again and again and again, for only when Spirit is acknowledged in physical reality can physical reality become Spiritual expression.

W: Bless you, Emmanuel, for being in my reality.

E: Beautiful love.

< 25 >

DIALOGUE FIVE

17 March 1978

W: All sorts of good things have been happening, Emmanuel, since I last saw you. First some thoughtful friends offered me their apartment in Honolulu, so in mid-January I packed my juicer and all the organic food I could carry and happily abandoned the snow and slush of New York for the sunshine and ocean breezes of Hawaii, where I kept busy with my healing program, which now included sunbathing and walks along the beach, and most of the time I found myself feeling very positive about the way things were going. And now after being back only a few days I'm off for Florida and a Spiritual Retreat Center near Vero Beach where they have opened their hearts to me.

E: You have experienced the true gentleness of Life in the past crisis and in walking the path that you have chosen, and it has touched upon an echoing gentleness within your own Being that, you have discovered, has tremendous resiliency. It is the power of Surrender, it is the true strength, and there is no longer any need for substitutes.

< 26 >

My dear friend, you have stood upon the rock and found yourself saved. There will now be a sureness in your step, the light of Truth in your eyes, and a forcefulness in your love that will brook no interference in the furthering of your Soul's purpose. A student dies and a Teacher is born, it is an act of transformation, and you should now stand ready to do battle for those who will come to you, to advise, to lead, to persuade, to counsel those who are seeking the solidity that you have found.

For is not Life in its process a battle between the positive and negative aspects, between sickness and health, between good and evil? My friend, the lines of reality have been clearly drawn for you. Through your past experience you are learning the power of Surrender. You know the power of meditation. You know the power of hope and the determination of commitment. These are the weapons, if you will, that the battle for Light and for goodness can be won by. And when I say "battle," I speak not only in metaphoric terms but also in very realistic ones, for those who come with faint heart and no hope require an ally such as you, one who has gone through the fire of doubt and of illness and has come out victorious. You are a Teacher, and as a Teacher, make no mistake, you are the warrior.

W: The gentle warrior.

E: Yes, and there is much in the plan of Salvation that requires such as you. In your gentleness and in your understanding, my friend, is your true strength, but do not hesitate to show anger when you feel that it is necessary. Indeed, anger in the service of Truth is a very

< 27 >

powerful and a very righteous weapon. Jesus was certainly angry when he threw the money changers out of the temple, and on many other occasions as well that are not recorded.

It is a time for action. It is time to trumpet what you know to your blessed world. There is no longer any need for you to walk with timidity or unsureness. You are more than adequately structured to grow and to prosper, and most certainly, as you have found, to survive and to do battle for others. The time of feasting is here, the time of rejoicing, the time of reaping the harvest. Do not hesitate to put your scythe to the ripening grain. It is yours, my friend. You have paid the price.

W: I'm ready, Emmanuel, I'm more than ready, although I'm sure there will still be moments when some of the old anxiety creeps back in to spoil the celebration.

E: Did you hear us speak to you in your times of concern? We did, you know, and many other times as well.

W: Not in so many words, Emmanuel, but I was certainly aware of your love and support, especially when I meditated. I had pillows around me, not so much for you and the other members of our Soul Family to sit on as to help me attune to your presence. Your pillow was right next to mine, and at times I had a real sense that you were with me, and it was very comforting. But then just recently there's been a lot of doubt and wondering if you weren't just a figment of my wishful thinking, and it's made me feel really disconnected.

< 28 >

E: Rest assured, my dear friend, that I was indeed there beside you, and your feeling of being disconnected does not in any way alter that reality. I would also like to assure you that even though we have all connected many times in our Consciousnesses, this does not mean that you cannot stand or function without us. This is of extreme importance at this stage of your growth, for as you assume the mantle of Teacher and put aside the schoolbooks of the student you assume also the responsibility of being the initiator of communication, not only with those in your physical reality but with us who are in Spirit as well.

In other words, as you assume the role of Spiritual Teacher—of earth Master, if you will—there is a need for you to assume also the initiative, the authority, the joy, the creativity of your expanded Being, and therefore as you wish us to communicate with you, bid us welcome and trust that you will be aware of our presence. It need not be in a visual form or in an audible form, but simply in the knowing that we are there.

I thank you for the special place you have set aside for me, and I have occupied it from time to time and will again most certainly. But there are others in Spirit form that are around you and that will continue to be around you in an expanding and alternating circle who yearn to connect with you and to communicate with you and to work with you in a very close and intimate way. These need to have room made for them also, and so I suggest that you leave the space next to you vacant for whoever wishes to occupy it and that you then let go of your concepts, be open, and attune yourself to whatever vibratory energy is sitting next to you. And remember that we are friends, so greet us as friends.

< 29 >

W: As partners?

E: Yes, as partners. As companions, as kinsmen—that is a strange concept, is it not, kinsmen in the Spirit world?—and allow us into your life as though we were in actual physical bodies. Indeed, there are those of us who have from time to time been with you in physical form, as you are already well aware, but there are others who have never been human and have therefore been with you only during your interim periods. Oh yes, my dear friend, there are Souls who do not need to come into physical form, and yet they exist as clearly as you and I do; they exist to assist as we do. They simply have not found it necessary to go through the depths of learning that we have, for they did not pull away as far or as vehemently or for as long a time as we did.

They do not want to be worshipped, nor do any of us. We want to be heard and we want to be spoken to just as you do. Worship belongs to only One, and that One is God. All Souls, with few exceptions, are equal in their yearning, in their value, in their structure, and as you envision yourself at the core of this very active learning process our connection will grow and deepen and you will find that you are able to give to those who come to you whatever it is that they are in need of.

Again, you are quite capable, as you know, of functioning in human form without guidance. You have earned this through lives of toil and suffering and learning, and this is most certainly a time for self-trust and self-discovery and self-expansion. And yet the guidance is always there for you. It will come through as Intuition, it can come through as knowing, it can come through your sleep state, and it can come directly

< 30 >

or indirectly, as it is coming at this moment. Rest assured that the sense of disconnection you spoke of is only temporary. It is just that you have been enveloped in a physical crisis which has given you much material for learning, a wealth of experience, but has not destroyed your connection with Spiritual Reality. It has only refocused you for a time where the focus was necessary.

There is no difference between the physical and the Spiritual Realities, there is no line of demarcation, there is no unfortunate duality. All things are One, and your Spirit companions are always with you. If you are not able to be aware of this, it is not because they do not wish to be known but because there is some resistance in you which is all very much involved with the growth process of becoming the Teacher and which is making it difficult for you to connect with them. We rejoice with you, my friend. The best is yet to come.

W: That sounds like your last word, Emmanuel, or is there perhaps something more?

E: Perhaps a closing sentence or two. As a tree grows tall, the roots grow deep and strong and wide. Let your humanness become part of your strength.

W: That's right out of my book, Emmanuel.

E: I said it was a partnership, did I not? God bless you, my friend.

< 31 >

DIALOGUE SIX

28 April 1978

E: Did you think, my dear Wingate, that having leaped the hurdle of this past experience trusting completely in the will of the Soul, did you think for one moment that you had taken the final step and that your work in this life was finished? Nothing could be further from the truth. This is not a time of ending but of a new beginning. You have seen the Cross upon the Hill, symbolizing the ultimate goal, the perfect weaving together of the physical with the Spiritual Realities so evident in the life of Christ, and you are heading for it.

You are now ready to begin again on a completely new plateau of understanding to redo the structure of your life, listening to the inner wisdom as it comes to you from deeper and ever deeper levels of Truth, far deeper than you ever imagined they could be. Go back and revitalize all that you have done to this point, not in a strenuous way but in accordance with your newfound wisdom and faith. Begin writing again, and we who draw near to you in the name of Truth and in the name of God to deliver the message that humanity needs to hear will speak to you. Simply leave yourself open, and

< 32 >

if the inspiration that comes to you is not in the vein that you choose to have it or it is not what you want to say, then do not use it. You have the right of editorship in all things.

It is also vitally important for you to go over and over again your past experience, not in a morbid way but rather in a way of openness to receive whatever there is, to learn from it, and then to pass this on to others. So much has happened on so many levels, not only the physical, the mental, the emotional, and the spiritual, but also in subtle gradations of these levels.

You are well, my friend, so look then to the future as a whole man.

W: Bless you, Emmanuel, for walking beside me. I don't know what I would have done without your love and guidance. And yes, I do feel that I've been victorious the way you said I would be. And I feel that as I continue with my program a lot of other good things are going to start happening to me. Already my heart center is opening up, the anger in my belly is gone, I'm more supple, my reaction time is much faster, and I don't know when I've had so much energy and vitality.

But my weight is of growing concern to me. I'm down to one hundred twenty-five pounds now, which is thirty pounds less than what I used to weigh in January, and I seem to be putting almost as much time and effort into getting back those lost pounds as I did in getting my cancer under control.

E: When one begins the process of detoxifying the physical body there are tremendous changes that take place; indeed, some of them, and I have said this before,

< 33 >

will seem to be more of a problem than the original toxicity itself. But may I also point out that along with the benefits you are already aware of you have also avoided a severe condition of arthritis of the spine. Indeed, if you had had X rays taken before and after— which of course you did not and would not do, for they would be poisonous to you—you would have found a tremendous difference in them. There has also been a releasing of lactic acid stored deep in the musculature of your body, which, of course, is the reason you are finding yourself more supple, and I suggest that these residual blessings of the cleansing process be used in your writing and in your teaching.

W: So now to work, and it's a good thing I'm so full of energy, because there is indeed much work to do. For example, all the energy has gone out of the Growth Center as a result of my being away most of the time since early January. And now there's really nobody coming to it anymore, maybe two or three people occasionally. The rest wandered off while I was so totally preoccupied with other things, and I can't say that I blame them. And I need to spend time, as you have suggested, going over what's been happening to me and fitting the pieces into the jigsaw puzzle of my spiritual truths and realizations and revitalizing all that I have done, especially the book, which I haven't even looked at since last fall.

And today I found myself driving up to Connecticut early so I would have time to look at land, all because of a vision I kept having when I was in Hawaii of a Growth Center Farm where there would be an opportunity for tilling the soil as well as *Tilling the Soul.*

< 34 >

E: I wish to caution you that this experience of what you feel is an oncoming truth means simply that you are being made aware of what will evolve, or has great possibility of evolving in the future, but it does not really mean that you should begin to structure it now. Rest in the wisdom as you are doing that when something is to be it will be, and that yes, if you choose to look at property that is all well and good, but, my dear friend, this is truly not the time to begin to expand so widely. Begin at the beginning, as we have said, and as we both understand it, with the revision of your inner reality and the inclusion of that revision in your creative work, which will then grow of its own impetus. And then one day there will come a surge of need, and when that time comes the land will be there, you will not have to seek it.

W: What about my playing golf, Emmanuel? I wonder if I have the time for it anymore, what with all the other things I have to do.

E: There is a tendency in all of you who feel the calling to serve God to hasten quickly and to wish at one level or another to put your physical needs aside and serve and only serve.

The attitude is beautiful, but the truth is quite different, for as physical beings you have needs, and these needs extend across the board, and to give yourself enjoyment, even of the frivolous kind, is very necessary.

So do not tie yourself, do not blind yourself to your work. If you feel that you need to exercise by playing golf and attacking the logistical problems of that sport,

< 35 >

then by all means you should do it. You will not be wasting time, for it will be feeding your Soul in another way. So give yourself permission to enjoy this particular pursuit of yours. It is most certainly approved by God.

W: But with this program I'm on, I get up and start running at six o'clock in the morning and I'm still running when I go to bed at eleven o'clock at night. How can I justify all the hours I spend playing golf?

E: My friend, now that you have to a great extent achieved your health you need to maintain it and enjoy it, and not drive it into the ground again. Whenever you feel the urge to tie yourself in one way or another to your task, step back a bit, take a different perspective, and ask the part of you that is rushing, that is so intent upon accomplishment in your physical sense, ask that part what it thinks of God's timeless Universe.

W: I am very tied to time.

E: I realize that.

W: All my life I've made a big deal out of getting wherever I'm going on time, or finishing whatever I'm doing on time.

E: Don't scoff at that training. There is no discipline, no matter how strange, how strict, how senseless it may seem, that does not have its value in a very positive way, but it is time to let that one go.

< 36 >

W: I do find that I'm flowing much more. I'm not breaking down doors the way I used to, for example. Most of the time they seem to be already open, and if they aren't, I just walk away.

E: Or you can just walk through the wall.

W: Not yet, Emmanuel, but it does seem as though things are coming more easily now. Maybe it's because I'm letting things happen instead of trying to make them happen, the way I always used to.

E: Exactly, and when you get to a point where all things are flowing, which I feel you are very close to, and your life has finally become aligned with Truth and there are no obstacles and you have accepted your humanness, then the struggle to perfect yourself as a human being will be over and you will again be given the choice of whether you will leave to serve on the other side of physical reality or continue in this lifetime, which in all probability you will choose to do.

< 37 >

DIALOGUE SEVEN

28 July 1978

E: You seem to be facing another time of crisis, my dear friend. Is this not so?

W: Yes, Emmanuel, it's a healing crisis at last, and it seems to have the potential for being a truly monumental one. At least the naturopathic doctor I've been going to says he's never in his thirty-five years of practice seen so much poison come out of any body as is coming out of mine, especially my right lung, and I'm already so weak that I wasn't sure I was going to be able to make it up here.

E: I know, dear Wingate, but there is nothing to fear, do you hear me? There is nothing to fear. Oh, you will say to me that you are not afraid, that this crisis is something you have long sought and that it signifies the culmination of your healing efforts. And yet there is a part of you that is afraid, and it is this that is pulling energy away from you that you so dearly need. If you will accept that part and learn to feel it and express it,

< 38 >

you will find that you are again renewed in your seeming battle for survival.

You have come a long way, a long, long way, and it has been many months that have brought you to this crisis. Listen now to the voices of love that surround you and have surrounded you during your entire life. Let your yearning speak and your hope flower. This is not the time for faint heart but absolute faith. It is a time of decision, a most wondrous time, your Soul is evolving so rapidly. If you could but see the light as we see it, my dear, dear friend, you would rejoice.

W: I do rejoice, Emmanuel, and don't worry, I'm going to stay with this healing crisis until it is finished, no matter what. I've gone through too much to get to this point to stop now.

E: What you are experiencing is the end of the battle. You have made the decision to stay, and although there is still a small area left that is saying "I'm tired of this, why don't I go home," your Life Force is saying "I want to stay, there is much still to do here," and that is much the stronger. It is now simply a matter of assuming the posture of staying, which is to begin to consciously take command of your life. You have worked through the small will, you have worked through the ego will, although you are afraid you have not; you sense a vestige, but do not be too harsh on yourself. It is only the Higher Will that is expressing Itself through you now, and if there is indeed a shadow of that ego will that you came into this life to understand and to utilize for its express purpose and then to blend with the

< 39 >

Higher Will, so be it. Just don't throw the baby out with
the bath water, don't insist upon perfection, but begin
instead to assert your Higher Will and flow with the
positive aspect of deciding what you want and claiming
the supremacy of your Soul's decision.

Now I am not suggesting, dear Wingate, that you will
be sanctified in this lifetime—you have never wanted
that anyway—but you *are* entering a level of evolvement
where you are becoming totally aware of your role as
the creator of your life. A wondrous time, a wondrous
time. Open your heart to this knowing and allow
yourself to accept it.

You still feel unworthy at times, and in that sense of
unworthiness your small ego is still alive. But once you
let go of the small will and you are one with God, then
there is no longer any ego or any sense of unworthiness
left. Gratitude perhaps, humility maybe, but also joy
and expansion and Self-awareness. Accept who you
are, Wingate, accept who you are. Accept your humanness as well as your Divinity, totally and without
reserve. Accept who you are, and the transformation
that you so earnestly wish for will take place. You are
safe. You know that, my friend, you are safe. I love you
too much not to speak the truth.

And now, if I may make a small suggestion, allow the
dear Soul who accompanied you to drive you back to
New York. She is comfortable with the car, and it is
better for you not to have the stress. And when you
reach home, lie on the floor where you are most sure
that the Divine Energies will come to you and communicate with your Consciousness, your Life Force, not
forcibly, but allowing what is there within you to gently
rise to the surface. And do not shut out the fear, do not

< 40 >

deny anything that seems negative to you. This is a time of growth, this is a time of housecleaning in a very real and beautiful sense.

And now, dear friend, in your vision imagine that we are holding hands and let us sit together for a few moments before you leave. But we will see each other many more times in this life.

< 41 >

24 August 1978

W: Thank you for coming down here this time, but I could never have made it up to Westport. I can't even make it off this couch I've been stranded on for three weeks now to get upstairs to bed, or anywhere else, for that matter. I have a fever that's been running well over a hundred, my weight is not much more—one sixteen and dropping fast—I cough much more of the time than I don't, and if I didn't have loving Souls to take care of me almost around the clock I don't know what I'd do.

It's all part of the healing crisis I'm having, I know that, and I'm sure that when it's finally over and the detoxification process has been completed my lake will be cleaner than ever. But it's heavy going, Emmanuel, lots heavier than I ever expected it would be, and I guess I very much needed a dear and trusted friend to tell me not to worry, that I was going to be all right.

E: The fever, my dear Wingate, is cleansing and purifying the parts of your physical body that you have wanted to cleanse and purify, and once this crisis has

< 42 >

been passed you will again be able to function as a whole and vitally alive human being.

But in your desire for transformation you are also attempting to burn something else out of you that does not need to be burned out. It needs to be accepted; your humanness, the things that you have abhorred in yourself. Transformation comes through self-acceptance, not through self-denial. It comes through acceptance of who you are as a man, as a human being, and yet here you are condemning yourself so severely that it has gotten to the point where you are punishing yourself almost to extinction. There is a need, indeed a necessity, for you to embrace yourself as you are now, at this moment, and then to have faith that once you embrace and love and understand yourself transformation will take place.

W: That shouldn't be all that difficult, Emmanuel, especially when you believe as I do that God is everyone and everything, including me, and that we are all part of the Divine Perfection. But some of the negative feelings I have about myself are so deep down that in many cases I don't even remember why I have them.

E: I know, dear Wingate, and in your present weakened state you feel reluctant to begin the inner search at that deeper level that claims not only your desire to be transformed but also your feeling that you are not worthy of being transformed as well. You have been told that you have given yourself over to the Will of God, but the Will of God is that you flourish in your

< 43 >

physical reality. Hold to this thought and never let it go, that where your heart is open to the Will of God, to your Higher Will, you will find wholeness and respite and peace, but where you are still battling in your human, in your ego will, you will find only pain and distress.

Your body is a battleground, dear Wingate, between two factions that are warring within you, the faction that wishes to do the Will of God and the faction that does not, the area within you that resists the Light and the area that strives to reach it. You have done the heavy work, but there is more, there are still hidden crevices, that vestige, if you will, that still does not wish to hear the totalness of God's Will, that is choosing rather to withdraw.

But, my friend, when one has chosen a life such as yours of ultimate purification, you must not stop at the doorway of Truth, you must advance in.

W: If I knew how to do it, Emmanuel, I would have done it a long time ago.

E: Let me suggest that you take the initiative to begin to explore that area within you that you have thought and that you have hoped was silenced and hear the voices that still rage beneath your awareness. There is an unwillingness there, an inability perhaps to understand completely the meaning of humanness and to accept that humanness in all its seeming imperfection and to open your heart to it.

Think about this. Indeed, there is much for you to think about, much for you to realize. Do you not see

< 44 >

how wisely you have manifested this crisis that is forcing you into immobility so that you have time to think, to contemplate? And you must if you are to cross the threshold we have spoken of in this lifetime.

Relive if you must one more time your infractions against Divine Law and see within each memory the light of the human being that in all its distortion was seeking Truth and yet clinging to the distortion. Do not see yourself in more than reality or in less than reality, but see yourself as a total Being and pray for the courage and the strength to give yourself forgiveness, complete love, acceptance. Only in this way will the toxicity of your body, which you are constantly feeding by your inner condemnation, be alleviated.

I stand by you, we all stand by you. You are cradled in the infinite love of God, and yet you must open your heart to your own humanness completely and totally in order for that love to heal you.

W: Thou shalt love thyself. I call this Commandment 2B, but it should probably be 1A. If you don't love yourself you can't very well love thy neighbor as thyself. And you certainly can't love God, who is not only in you as you but in your neighbor also.

E: Now rest, my dear friend, knowing that in your times of silence and meditation you are lifted, and that the communications you feel you experience in that lifted state are very real. It is a time of decision, dear Wingate, a most important time indeed, and if you will but see your physical body as merely an extension of the Soul, as the spoken word of your Being, then you will

< 45 >

be able to understand very clearly the circumstances in which you now find yourself.

Several days after this dialogue, Wingate was examined by his family doctor and advised that he had advanced pneumonia and that his vital signs were critically low and he had only days to live. Finally, he agreed to abort his healing crisis and go to the hospital for medical treatment.

Unlike the naturopathic interpretation of illness—which, as Wingate discussed with Emmanuel in Dialogue Four, holds that all sickness is caused by accumulated toxic waste within the body and that the way back to health, whatever the disorder, is through the elimination of the toxicity—the orthodox medical tradition defines illness according to the symptoms a body manifests, which can range anywhere from a sore throat to a malignant growth, then classifies the illness by a specific name, such as pneumonia or cancer, and generally seeks an antidote to the specific symptoms, which may entail the introduction of drugs, chemotherapy, radiation, and the like. In the healing crisis, the final stage of the naturopathic cure, in which the body is throwing off toxicity and returning to its natural state of health and vitality, a variety of physical reactions can occur, and Wingate's reactions of high fever, lung congestion, and overall weakness, though unusually severe, are not considered uncommon responses.

From the naturopathic viewpoint, the adminis-

< 46 >

tration of antibiotics, which were intravenously fed into Wingate for several weeks, worked against the elimination of the toxic matter from his body, and therefore terminated the healing crisis. From the medical viewpoint, on the other hand, the antibiotics were necessary to counter the infection and congestion in his respiratory system and cure the pneumonia.

In the hospital, X rays of his right lung revealed the presence of a fist-size mass, which, he was told by a lung specialist, was most likely malignant. And, for the first time since November, when the growth on his prostate was discovered to be cancerous, a concerned urologist at the hospital tried, unsuccessfully, to persuade him to have surgery, explaining that there was a strong probability it would metastasize and the cancer would spread to his spine.

Despite this, Wingate held firmly to his faith in Emmanuel's pledge that he would be victorious in his struggle, and to the healing program he had been following. After two biopsies failed to show any malignancy in his right lung, and the pneumonia was no longer a problem, and once again refusing to undergo prostate surgery, Wingate left the hospital, although still very weak and unable to get around without a wheelchair.

In October, he returned to the Spiritual retreat in Vero Beach to rest and recuperate and to resume a modified version of his healing program.

< 47 >

DIALOGUE NINE

2 February 1979

E: You have been through a great deal since you were last here, have you not, dear Wingate? But whatever the causes of your extreme crisis, the psychological reasons, the spiritual reasons, the medical reasons, it is not necessary now to understand them or to discern whether it was a healing crisis or whether it was the body calling for help through the vocabulary of a lung difficulty. It is enough that you are here and that you grew and you learned, and the causes are irrelevant.

And so to the future, and so to tomorrow. What shall it be, my friend, what shall it be? The entire Universe is at your disposal, quite literally. Oh yes, of course it is available to everyone, but so few know that. You have found it out through your recent struggle, so what shall it be? Settle for nothing less than what you truly desire, and do not be afraid to ask for what you feel will bring you joy and fulfillment.

Humility is not in being meek. Humility is in letting go of the small will, the conscious will, and adhering to the Universal Will. This is true humility, and it makes

< 48 >

you both humble and Master, for you then have become One with the Creator.

W: Very humbly, Emmanuel, what about my cancer, and how is it doing now that my healing crisis is over?

E: Cancer? My dear friend, the body has forgotten it. Put it aside, it is no longer essential. It can exist or not exist, as it chooses, but it is not going to be a problem for you, not anymore.

W: And so we live forever after in a state of friendly, peaceful coexistence. And I feel so vital again, Emmanuel, so full of energy, I don't know what I'm going to do with it all.

E: My friend, we were just speaking of that. Many of the things that we talked about last spring seemed at that time to be only a vision, a dream, an improbability, but as you reclaim your life the things that were touched upon then will become a reality. Before, you had not the strength to create a new purpose. You thought of it, you experienced it, although mildly, but you did not have the creative power available at that time to follow through with it. But you are fast becoming connected again with this power, and so your life will now begin to take on a new and expanded dimension.

You have been aware for some time that you have the ability to turn yourself over to an inner commitment, an inner light, an inner voice, an inner purpose. But there has also been a sense within you that you had to skirt fanaticism in your convictions and your belief systems,

< 49 >

and you have made very sure that you have been intellectually clear in order to achieve this. However, you are now coming to a point in your growth where the creative energy from these deep convictions can be blended and wedded with the mature mind, bringing together these two vital forces in a state of dynamic union.

W: Your use of the word *fanaticism* puzzles me, Emmanuel.

E: When I spoke of fanaticism perhaps I did use an unfortunate term. What I was speaking of is your deep caring, your desire to be totally immersed in your beliefs and to express them completely from the depths of your being without caution. And to use that part of the mind that has in the past been used to suppress or divert your passion to blend with it and to enhance it. And so the passion feeds the wisdom and the wisdom feeds the passion.

Through the eons that you have struggled to find the Light and to experience your unique Oneness with God and with Universal Love, you have many times touched, sometimes briefly and sometimes in an extended caress, the attributes of Truth and courage, regardless of what the consequences might be. Now you have come to the apex of this experiencing, of this learning process, and have vowed to speak your Truth. Oh yes, you will be called upon in this lifetime to avow your beliefs, publicly, openly, passionately. The time will come, have no fear of that, in a most natural and a most obvious way. Indeed, there are many enclaves of Souls that are seeking, each in a unique way, to grow,

< 50 >

to know, to discover, much as you in your Ministry are helping those who come to you; and, if you will forgive the prediction, all of this will blend in your lifetime and you will be called upon to speak and you will speak, my friend, make no mistake about that.

W: Meanwhile, dear Emmanuel, couldn't I be of greater service if there were more people coming to study with me?

E: They will gather now that your strength is gathering. And the book, the book will also bring them.

W: If I ever finish it. First the cancer, and now it seems as though I am constantly thinking of new things to say, or old things to say differently.

E: My friend, try not to keep altering your book to your total present understanding, because then you will be communicating only with people who are experiencing what you are experiencing. You are writing from many different levels of knowing, from many different levels of experiencing, for many, many people, and where one level may seem to you simplistic or limited, it will vibrate, it will ring, it will be a clear and gentle walkway in for those who are at that particular level of understanding. This is not the final and only statement you will ever make, so why not just think of it as Volume I and let your writing be a continuum, as your life is a continuum.

Do you mind if we look over your shoulder occasionally? We do, you know.

W: Of course not, Emmanuel. You know I don't. How do you think it's going?

< 51 >

W: It is indeed a most excellent work, and one in which we are all having a hand. Are you aware of our guidance?

W: Sometimes, Emmanuel. I just wish it could happen more often.

E: You receive it whenever you need it, but it would be an interference for you to receive strong guidance, or indeed guidance of any kind, when you are in the process of using your own considerable faculties. There would be a sense of confusion, and so let us not tamper with the way it is.

The work is going well, and you as human being, as a loving brother, are going well also. We rejoice for you. And now let us sit in silence for a moment and communicate at the deeper levels that we have experienced together, and then go your way with our love and blessings.

< 52 >

1 June 1979

E: There is such joy here, there is such joy at this moment in greeting you again, my dear friend, there is such a sense of shared adventure, you and I. How remarkably transparent the unnecessary barrier that is erected between one level of reality and another becomes, once one has flowed with Life and has experienced both the power of destruction and the power of realization and has touched the Spirit within. You are free, my friend, you are free.

W: Does everybody have to go through what I've just gone through to be free, Emmanuel?

E: In one way or another, yes, although perhaps not so harshly. And yet I feel you are still troubled by something, even though the reality is that you have nothing to worry about.

W: It's the book, Emmanuel. It's just going very, very slowly. And not only am I troubled, I also feel guilty about not getting it done by now.

< 53 >

E: My dear friend, this does not call forth the need for guilt. As you and I both know, guilt is the most destructive, the most useless and most stagnant energy of all. It serves no purpose and causes all things to glue to a stop, and is an encumbrance that is certainly no longer necessary in your life.

The sense of delay connected with this project is very much associated with a belief in a deep recess of your Being that if you do not have this to work on, then you will have nothing left to do. And so you are delaying its completion in a very human way, because there is a sense of dread at finishing the book at this time, as though you are afraid there are only a limited amount of things for you to do in this lifetime. You still have not accepted completely the reality of eternity, of open-endedness, and it would be very helpful for you in your private meditation if you were to practice seeing everything as limitless, as boundaryless.

W: I do remind myself from time to time of Volume II and Volume III and Volume IV and so on, and then there are all the other things that I now find myself involved in besides Volume I, like the almost daily Meditation Services that more and more students are coming to and the two-day Growth Course that I've been giving every few weeks and our regular monthly retreats. So it doesn't look as though I'm going to run out of things to do for a long, long time, but you're right, Emmanuel, there is a part of me, deep down where I'm hardly aware of it, that feels that once I've finished the work I've been given to do in this lifetime, well, that's it. And yet another part of me, even deeper down, knows that Life is eternal and everlasting and

< 54 >

that there is always more to do, there is always more to learn.

E: Exactly, and so you see, my friend, all you need to do when you have finished the work at hand is to ask what the next step is and then listen for the answer, which of course has already been programmed into your Soul and into your heart.

W: It's all there, isn't it, Emmanuel, right at the edge of my knowing?

E: Yes, my dear Wingate, and, as we both know, the ultimate lesson of every Soul is the total acceptance of God's Will as it manifests in an open heart. There, perhaps that will help you finish you book.

W: It will, Emmanuel, and I feel that getting it done is going to be a big step in energizing the work of the Growth Center.

E: Completing the book will be important in your Ministry, there is no question about that, but its importance for you now is not so much in its completion, except in the letting go of your misconception of finality, as it is the ongoing process of creating, and as you focus on that importance, then the finished product will have life and vitality and therefore be of greater value to those who will read it. In other words, it is the creative process of writing the book that is important, not the finishing of it.

Indeed, the period of intense creativity in which you are now involved is giving you the feeling of being very

< 55 >

much one with the God within you. Don't be afraid of this feeling. Don't try to humble it. It comes from a place of deep humility or you wouldn't be experiencing it. Trust it, and when you feel it clear, enjoy it and know that it is the Truth. It is who Mankind really is.

W: You know total Truth, don't you, Emmanuel, and it's probably there for all of us, if we could just get in touch with it. But then you can't show me what you feel I'm not ready to see, can you?

E: But this is most certainly not a conspiracy to keep you in ignorance, dear Wingate. The Truth is all there, to be sure, but you are able to be aware of only a part of It at this time, much as you can see only a part of the color spectrum, even though you know there is much more. However, as you expand your Consciousness more Truth will be there for you. Indeed, if you were to replay our present conversation at some future time you would hear things you are not perhaps yet ready to hear. But they are there, my friend, they are there.

And yes, I am schooled most carefully in the ability to perceive what you are able to absorb. Not what it is proper for you to hear, for total Truth is what is proper for you to hear, but what you are able to absorb. And you *are* opening up more and more, and you able to absorb more and more, and you do, as you already suspect deep within you, know the total Truth. You know God, you are God.

W: God is in me, as me. There are moments when I really experience that, Emmanuel, and then, of course, there are those other moments when I fall back into my unenlightened humanness.

< 56 >

E: And yet those moments when your inner vision becomes unclear is not a time for self-criticism, but a time for questioning as to why the blurring is happening, and whether there is still a vestige of disbelief.

W: And that's not the only blurring I'm having a problem with, Emmanuel. I'm having a problem with my physical vision, too, only that's blurred all the time now. I've been legally blind in my right eye since I was a boy, as the result of a post-trauma cataract, which wouldn't be all that much of a problem except that now a cataract is developing in my left eye as well, and I wonder if you can tell me why this is happening and what, if anything, I can do about it.

E: My friend, one must at times be in darkness in order to see Light, in sickness in order to know health, in despair in order to know joy, and in distortion in order to know Truth, and it is to bring about the inner knowing that this growth has become necessary. As a Soul you created the cancer in your physical body and then healed it, did you not, my friend? And as a Soul you are now creating this visual obstruction, first in an inner sense and then in a literal sense, but when the inner understanding reaches a point of true knowing then the outer body, albeit functioning at a much slower rate of perception than the inner sensing, will begin to change.

And may I suggest that you say to yourself over and over again—and you know, my friend, there is no demand in any of my suggestions, but only a direction for you to consider taking—say that you want to see everything, you want to see Life as it is, you want to see

< 57 >

total Truth, you want to see yourself in absolute clarity, you want to see your fellow humans in absolute clarity. Say that you want to see beauty, you want to see Light, you want to see God, even where you think there is ugliness, for even in ugliness there is a striving for Truth. Indeed, every Soul that has manifested in the physical world, whether It be in extreme distortion or not, has come through courage and love and has a beautiful Being in It.

W: You're a beautiful Being, Emmanuel, and I do believe that everyone and everything is part of God's perfection and a beautiful Being also, but it's one thing to believe it and another thing to feel it in my heart. You do, Emmanuel, you feel it in your heart, and you inspire me to become more and more like you. But even when I reach such a place of flowing acceptance where I see everyone as being just the way they are supposed to be, just the way God wants to be, in them as them, isn't it still my responsibility as a Teacher to see where those who come to me for advice are in error and to explain to them how this is not appropriate, or that should be done differently? Or should I simply say that this has been my experience, or this is my truth to accept or reject, and let it go at that?

E: The last approach is the more useful one, for as you very well know, dear friend, all you can truly offer anyone is your own truth, and whether others are able to follow that, whether it is indeed their truth also, is something everyone must decide for himself. Being a Teacher of Truth is being a radiant Light that some will

< 58 >

THE BOOK OF SURRENDER

see and some will not, and one of the difficulties of being a Teacher, of being in the service of God, is not having a sense of control. In humanness that is not always easy to accept, and yet if you know something is true, and you do indeed know many things are true, and if there are those who do not accept your truth, respect is still due them nevertheless.

This is not a carelessness of discipline. It is a matter of allowing each person their own truth, their own path. But if you feel that it is not appropriate for you to condone their thoughts or actions, then it is your right to encourage them to think or act differently, or simply to say "I withdraw." But as a Teacher you cannot say "Do this" or "Think that," you can only present yourself and offer your assistance and then be willing to let them go, knowing that they are not ready for your particular truth yet at the same time being open for them to return as well.

W: Thank you, Emmanuel, for reaffirming so beautifully things that I already know but sometimes forget that I know. In my teaching I always begin by saying that this is only *my* truth. That's there's no such thing as *the* Truth. There's my truth, and your truth, and perhaps our truth, and I gladly share mine with you, to accept or reject as you will.

E: Or use any part of it.

W: Yes, and use the rest as manure to grow truths and realizations that you like better.

E: That's ecologically very sound.

W: It's organic, too. For example, if something I say or write rubs someone the wrong way, like "There is only good, there is only God, and bad is only how you see those experiences whose part in your growth you do not yet understand," perhaps it will start them thinking about God again, and what they really feel God is, and what they feel God isn't. So many people these days think they have rejected God when they really haven't. They've just rejected the God they were brought up with, and perhaps this will start them thinking about what kind of God they *can* believe in.

E: That's a remarkable concept, worded in a very beautiful way. It will have an impact.

W: I know this is going from the sublime to the ridiculous, Emmanuel, but I wonder if you can tell me how long I'm going to be living and doing my thing where I am now.

E: My friend, being where you are is very important for the balance of Light and energy and truth in your dear city. Let me remind you that a doctor isn't needed where everyone is well. You have a function right where you are now. A very important function.

W: I like to think of the Growth Center as being like a lighthouse and that it's giving people a sense of comfort and direction.

E: Trust that.

W: That's what the English would call a Power Point.

< 60 >

E: Indeed, each Soul as it becomes lighted becomes a Power Point.

W: Yes, and what an incredible Power Point of Love and Light you are, dear Emmanuel. It's such a joy to be with you, such a joy.

E: Thank you, my brother, you have a lot of Light and beautiful things to be with, too. And together, someday, we will save the world, is that not so?

< 61 >

DIALOGUE ELEVEN

28 September 1979

E: The visions that have just been presented to you through my channel, my dear Wingate, are not some outer reality but are, in a very real sense, voices from your own inner being. The struggling is within you, the abundance is within you, the voice of wisdom is within you, the high, softly rolling field abundant with flowers is within you, and the winged Spirit that stands there is part of your own Higher Consciousness.

You are truly coming together within yourself, dear friend. Your physical self and your spiritual self are meeting and blending and becoming One, and although you are still in time, while I am in Eternity, we understand each other, you and I, and our kinship grows with each communication. Do you sense it?

W: Yes, Emmanuel, and as a way of increasing my awareness of your vibration I've been playing the tapes of our past dialogues every morning when I wake up and every night when I go to bed.

< 62 >

E: And yet to discern me as separate entity, as you do, is to put another reality on what is really there. The reality is that as you open yourself to me and I to you we are literally, in an energy sense, in a blessed sense, in a physical sense, One, and there is no differentiation between us.

W: *Namaste* says that so well, Emmanuel. It's a word they greet each other with in India that, roughly translated, means "I honor that place in you where, when you are in that place in you and I am in that same place in me, there is only one of us."

E: Exactly, but you who are in your physical reality seldom experience this Oneness with each other.

W: I do sometimes in our meditations at the Center, just for a flickering.

E: At those moments when you do, my friend, you are released from the illusion of your physical reality, your separateness, and you are in total Truth.

W: There was a time when I clung to my separateness, my sense of selfness, and would have fought tooth and nail to keep it. But now I can't wait to get rid of it so I can have my truth and my Oneness, especially with you and the other Souls who are with us. And there are times when I feel I'm really making progress, Emmanuel, and then something happens or someone says something like the other day that makes me so painfully aware of my physical reality again and my big clay feet and my separation. It's very discouraging.

< 63 >

E: Do not be upset, my dear brother, by how dualistic you have been caused to find yourself, or how dualistic each human being can be, or indeed how dualistic your dear planet is, but instead look at an experience such as this with an open heart and a yearning for growth. And I do wish to remind you, though perhaps needlessly, that you are here to grow, and when you are shown that there is indeed something that does not meet your idealized image of yourself, do not be overwhelmed but be grateful and rejoice, for there is a battlement that is being destroyed, and in the process you are moving closer to the Oneness that you have expressed such a desire for. And if you also find that you are not as removed from your own criticism as you would wish to be, then that too can be a blessing. You are still in a physical body, dear Wingate, do you hear me, you are still in a physical body, and you are therefore still in need of growth. And when you find yourself reacting as you had not envisioned yourself reacting, light a candle in the name of Truth and say "Ah yes, there I am with my humanness, which is beautiful and spontaneous and vital and alive and terribly necessary," and take the image that you hold of yourself as being above the criticism of others as well as of yourself and give it a decent burial.

W: But I'm sure a small frog in a small pond, Emmanuel, which would be all right if you were to tell me that that's the way it's supposed to be. But somewhere I've gotten the feeling, and I'm not sure that you're not responsible for at least part of it, that I'm not supposed to be such a little frog. As a matter of fact, last time we were here together you even said, and it didn't sound as

< 64 >

if you were just joking, that we would someday save the world together.

E: Indeed, I did say that we would someday save the world together, and I was not "just joking." Let me clarify that. Though my pleasure in your company does at times bring out a humorous area of communication, there are also very serious realities that we speak of, you and I, and this was most certainly one of them. But when I said we will save the world, I did not envision you on a mountaintop calling forth the forces of good and evil, if you will forgive me for using that unfortunate word. World leadership has never been to your liking, but neither were you meant to remain in the shadows, not at all. However, in the type of Ministry that you have chosen, in the type of Service, it may be months, it may be years, and indeed in some circumstances it could be lifetimes before the full extent of the contribution you have made is recognized. Indeed, those who are near to you and who need to experience what you have to give, which is nothing more nor less than your own truth, may not even within themselves recognize the full extent of your influence, either in this life or even in lives beyond. But I do say to you that the truths that you present will have the effect of a pebble dropped in water, where the ripples will spread and spread and spread, and in this way we will indeed save the world.

And so the seeking to find where you are remiss, my dear Wingate, must become a thing of the past. You most certainly have done all that you were required to do, and your self-criticism serves you no longer in any way. Indeed, the responsibility for the tilling of your

< 65 >

own Soul has been excellently recognized, and to look any longer for rocks in a field that has been tilled and tilled again is to focus on the minutiae rather than on the grander scale of things. Of course you will stumble on your humanness from time to time, and why not? Indeed, how could others speak to you or hear you if you did not have your own human imperfections? Why, you would be worshipped rather than recognized, and the time for worship of another human being has long since come and gone, and it is now time for the message to become very clear that you are not only as I am but that the sum total of all of us is Oneness with God.

W: You've been very comforting and reassuring, Emmanuel, and you've certainly given me a much clearer sense of purpose, but I know that there are going to be times in the future when I will still be confused as to whether what I'm doing is in accordance with God's Unfolding Plan.

E: It is only when you question what your heart is telling you that the confusion will come, but as your faith in your own Being and your own Truth is strengthened you will realize that what your deepest, profoundest desires dictate is indeed the Will of God.

W: Yes, yes, I forget that, Emmanuel, I forget that. It's even part of my teaching, that our deepest desires are but a lower vibration of the One Will, perfectly expressing Itself in us and through us.

E: And so the confusion is not grounded, is it?

W: And I talk about practicing what I teach. I guess I don't always do it, do I?

< 66 >

E: My dear Wingate, you're not expected to, always. But you do know Truth, you do know the Will of God, and it is a matter now of learning to accept it, which is always the difficult part, and to trust what you know and glory in it.

W: Thank you, dear Emmanuel, and bless you for your wisdom and your guidance.

E: Bless you, dear friend. It is always such a pleasure speaking with you. I enjoy the weaving together of our thoughts into different forms to bring about a deeper understanding, and while I have spoken to you and am still speaking to you through my channel, I also communicate with you through your own awareness and your own perception. Indeed, I am no closer to my channel than I am to you. We are all One, dear Wingate, and when you have finally completed this physical life we will meet again in an even closer and more personal relationship.

W: What a wonderful thing to look forward to, Emmanuel, but meanwhile there are all those pebbles to be dropped, so to work, to work.

< 67 >

DIALOGUE TWELVE

February 1980

E: Are you aware, my dear Wingate, of the new areas of experience that you are now moving into? Even as I speak to you there is an awakening taking place that is enabling you to be conscious of my presence in a deeper sense than you have previously experienced it.

Do not force yourself to be aware of this. It is not a matter of setting the stage through desire or belief and then envisioning my presence. It is simply a matter of being willing to accept my word that in your growing posture as a Teacher, you are opening your channel, your receptivity, and that you are able to receive directly the communication that is here for you and to give it directly to others. And if you are to fulfill your Soul's mission, then you must allow for this very advantageous step to take place.

W: Will I be conscious that I'm receiving your guidance, Emmanuel, or will I just find myself saying things without realizing they are coming from you?

< 68 >

E: You could experience it as intuitive knowing, as you suggest, but you are certainly able at this time to connect directly with me and the Spirits who are with you, and indeed all of your work in the future can be touched by this Divine guidance. But I want to urge you not to allow things to become complicated, and if you feel that you are not receiving the guidance that you need for a fellow traveler, then close your eyes and go deeper within yourself to that level of Soul Consciousness which you have so amply asked for and struggled to achieve and question why you are not receiving it, and then allow the answer to come. Simply accept the reality that the guidance is there and that you can receive it, and we will most certainly be with you in your growth process to assist you in whatever way we can.

W: And yet here I am, Emmanuel, feeling very bogged down and wondering when if ever I'm going to take my next step.

E: I know, my friend, but do not think even for a moment that your growth has stopped. Nothing could be further from the truth. Every plateau of what seems to be the closing of a circle is always the opening to another step forward, and as you move into these new and expanded areas of growth you will find that you are answering a very important question for a great many people, for you will be challenging the illusion that often exists in your dear humans that once you have accomplished something of major proportions, then the only step left is to die physically.

< 69 >

W: And that's so sad, Emmanuel, because those later years can be so important, so rewarding—at least they have been for me.

E: Yes, but this has been spoken of so fatuously so many times and there have been so many platitudes and Pollyanna euphemisms spoken in the name of truth that many older people find themselves in the depths of despair. And so, you see, there is tremendous work that needs to be done here in the communication of what you know to be truth based on your own experiences.

W: But at least for the moment, Emmanuel, it seems that my interest is primarily with the young.

E: Of course, my friend, because there is a part of you that is eternally young and there is a great love and excitement in this association, there is a great attractiveness in the greenness, the lushness of youth, and in planting a deeper and more profound truth in the rich soil. But that same richness and lushness can belong to all ages, and perhaps your next work can also be directed to retilling the soil of those who feel that their earth has been depleted and to planting in their gardens a deeper and more profound truth also.

You have done it for yourself, and this is certainly the first and most important step in doing it for others. But with such stress on aging as a negative function in your world, with all the confusion and dismay, all the unnecessary suffering and anguish, and with such a deep distrust of God and of a benign Universe and a reasoned and balanced nonchaotic Reality, you can see that you have your work cut out for you. There are

< 70 >

many, many facets of this, most of which are already familiar to you, and if you will but follow your heart, your good intent will flower into your next contribution. Certainly the book that you have written will, in its directness and clarity, help many, regardless of age, to open doors that have heretofore been shrouded in mystery.

W: And how do you like the book, Emmanuel, now that it is finally finished?

E: It is a great pleasure, my dear friend, not only to experience the physical manifestation of your efforts, which must truly give you great joy, but I am also pleased and humbled by your dedication.

W: Will the book really be successful, Emmanuel? Will it really help people?

E: Without question, and not only the more spiritually evolved, but those who are still struggling in their humanness as well. You know you speak truth. You have given with your heart and with your clarity and directness. You have given from your experience and your faith. What other ingredients are necessary?

W: It's been suggested that I publish it myself, Emmanuel. This feels very right to me, but I wonder how you feel about it.

E: That is totally out of the question. It will cause you unnecessary concern and keep you from your next step.

< 71 >

W: That's a surprise, Emmanuel. And a disappointment, too. I've found myself really enjoying the prospect of getting involved in the logistics of design and printing and distribution and things like that.

E: It most certainly is not wrong to relish and enjoy, but when that is used as a buffer perhaps to the next step, and there is an element here, which of course you are not conscious of, that is saying "This is successful and joyous and I wish to stay with it," then it is time to let your offspring grow up. It is time to let it go. This will enable you to be open to the future, which is most certainly on your doorstep at the moment, and the new guidance that is coming to you.

W: Hopefully it will not be always so strongly worded as the guidance you have just given me, Emmanuel, or quite so hard to take.

E: My dear Wingate, when I make such a strong statement I do not do it to direct your life. I by no means give orders, as you know. It is not my position, it is not my place, I did it as a way of getting you to focus on the deeper reality of the situation in which you now find yourself.

W: Oh, Emmanuel, you know that when you speak I listen, and that I'm not going to disregard what you said about not publishing the book. I can't.

E: And I thank you, my friend, for your willingness to put aside your efforts in that direction. And now if you will put them forth instead in the more expanded

< 72 >

arena in which you are finding yourself, you will find that the new guidance that is willing to come to you as well as the other aspects of your growth in this area will very quickly manifest and your new work will indeed begin.

< 73 >

DIALOGUE THIRTEEN

18 April 1980

E: There is a heaviness about you this morning, my dear Wingate, which I am sure you are only too well aware of.

W: And it's a feeling I've had off and on for as long as I can remember, Emmanuel.

E: I know, my friend, I know, and it is all part of a natural reluctance you dear Souls have to the inevitability of the evolutionary process. But your life is not something that flows in a haphazard way. Indeed, the groundwork for your present incarnation was laid centuries past, and the flow has been there through Eternity.

W: The Unfolding Plan.

E: Exactly, and when a Soul enters into the conscious struggle to reunite with God, there is then at that moment of Soul decision a path laid out in Infinity that says, "This is the way I will go, for that is where I want

< 74 >

to be." After the initial fact of making that fundamental Soul statement, all lives and all experiences within each life yield to that central theme, and so it is with you. Rest with this, rest with this, my friend, and appreciate the magnitude of the growth that has taken place in your life.

W: But am I really fulfilling my destiny, Emmanuel? And the reason I keep harping on this is that over the years so many people have predicted such terrific things for me, and it doesn't seem as though it's really happening, and I can't help but still feel guilty and questioning about what it is I haven't done that I should have done or what I've done that I shouldn't have done, and it's not a very good feeling. And yet here you are speaking of how extraordinary my growth has been in this lifetime, while I'm putting myself down for not having done enough.

E: And for not having fulfilled what have been other people's demands on you. But who can do that to you, my friend? Who can say to you, "Ah, you have greatness and this is how it must manifest itself"? It is quite strenuous enough what you demand of yourself. And yes, I am indeed addressing myself to this thought within you, for it is one that has plagued you for quite some time, and I wish to clarify, if I may, this situation so that it need no longer become a concern, or a weight, or in any way a deterrent to your real and natural growth.

What does it mean, this greatness that was predicted? Oh, I am not speaking to your conscious mind. Of course, you are completely reasonable and sane and

< 75 >

know perfectly well at that level that one person's mediocrity is another one's greatness. But what does it mean to you deep within you, this onus you place upon yourself of not fulfilling what you feel or have been told to believe is your Destiny in this lifetime? Destiny is the Soul's Consciousness flowing ever and ever more strongly and swiftly toward Light and toward Truth and toward Oneness. There is no other Destiny than this.

In the beginning of your Soul's awakening consciousness there was a Soul commitment that said "I want to go from my separateness and from my darkness and from my fear. I want to go to my Oneness and my Light and my Peace," and all lives have been lived for that purpose and no other. Oh, to be sure, in the conscious mind there have been small storms, much turbulence at times, much seeking, much failure, much fulfillment. But we are speaking of a deeper awareness that you are becoming more and more acquainted with, more and more comfortable with.

Look at yourself, my friend, look at yourself and see yourself as the human being that you are. Do you not see the magnificence there? I cannot believe that you don't. It is only false modesty that prevents you from saying "Yes, I have achieved wondrous things, and I am a glowing and beautiful example of God manifest in human form." The gifts that you give others I cannot even begin to enumerate. And yet there is this perfectionism that causes you to disregard what you do give, and to plague yourself to give what it is impossible for any human being to give.

But who demands perfection, my friend? Only you Souls who are locked in human form and who believe somehow that this is the requirement for Oneness with

< 76 >

God. It is not. The requirement is sincerity and an open heart. That is the perfection that is demanded. The perfect longing, the fully realized desire. Beyond and above that all is superfluous. Packaging, if you will, packaging. And the packaging of and by itself is really not bad. It is the underneath essence of your Being that I wish to direct your attention to, for your sense of unfulfillment is cruelly self-inflicted and need not be there at all.

Now I am not saying to you to stop growing, stop living, you have done your part. I am not saying that, for there is never a moment when Consciousness ceases its expansion. There is never a moment when life ceases in or out of the body, when yearning ceases, or when responsibility for one's fellow human ceases. Never. And once this realization is clearly imprinted on the Soul's Consciousness it goes on and on through Eternity. But I do say to you to look at what you have done, for only in seeing where you have been and what you have done can you begin to build for the future.

Accept a job well done, my friend. Put down the burden that you insistently assume and accept what has been accomplished as accomplished. You have fulfilled what you have been meant to fulfill to this point in your life. You have shirked very little, and where you have turned your back, as all humans do, you have chastised yourself so severely that one could not possibly say another word. The full measure has been exacted, and anything further tends a little toward the indulgent self that demands and demands and admonishes and admonishes, rather than accepting your humanness, your imperfection, and saying "Well, and so this is what I

< 77 >

have done. Is that not remarkable?" rather than "Look what I have not done."

Oh, to be sure, there is more, as I have said. There is always more. The creative spark is always flaring up and going back and flaring up and going back. It is much like the flame of a candle that, as the door of Consciousness opens and more air comes in, gathers strength and illuminates more of the darkness and then, as it settles into its next phase of growth and progress, seems to go back down again. But it only seems to because you have become accustomed to the added light. And then the door of your Consciousness opens again, and then more air comes in and more light flares up and more is illuminated. It is an eternal process.

W: Thank you, dear Emmanuel, and bless you, but I still can't help but ask myself, "What's the matter with you, Wingate? Why aren't you able to be more and do more?"

E: I know, I know. We hear that demand that you place upon yourself so unjustly. Let me speak more about this. For again, as I have already said, the burden that you place upon yourself is cruel and unjust, unnecessary and limiting, limiting in the fact of its demand, the demand that takes your time and attention and therefore robs you of the growth that you are yearning for. It is like a vicious circle.

There is a sense of unreality in all of this, and I would like to address myself to that, for the reality is that the crux of giving service is the heart. It is enough to be a loving and a caring man. Oh yes, I know, you have imperfections, but the fundamental issue here is not

< 78 >

your imperfections but your love. And when you can find that love and truly feel it I want you to vow to yourself time and time again that that is enough, for until you can accept that, my dear Wingate, you lock the doorway to the expansion you so dearly yearn for.

Now I do not mean that you are to put aside your desires for spiritual communication, your desires for inspirational guidance. I do not mean that at all. But your deep love and caring is what draws others to you—not the guidance, not the Divine Inspiration, but Wingate the man, Wingate the caring human being. This is so rare that those who know you want to warm themselves at the hearth of your inner caring. This is enough. How often can I say this?

And when you truly feel that caring, which often-times you do not, you place such demands on yourself to be more that you cannot feel the warmth of your own heart, but when you do allow yourself to feel it and to believe it—and to believe it is of utmost importance— then the rest will be open to you. For you will have learned the power of human love and the human heart, and this, of and by itself, is the agent that can bring Divine Inspiration and Divine Guidance. And do not put me off by saying "But who am I, a man, to suggest to others how they should live when I look at my life?" and I say to you, you are Wingate and you are a loving Soul.

There is no question that you do receive inspirational guidance. There is no question that this Divine Guid-ance will be with you continually and in ever-increasing volume and clarity, and the lack that you feel is quite simply because you believe that being who you are is not enough.

< 79 >

My dear, dear friend, when one speaks of humility, it is not the mock humility that is so often stressed in Biblical teachings by those who attempt to interpret them. It is simply to see yourself as the striving and beautiful Soul that you are and to accept that and not to demand that you be more than that, for there is no more than that. There is no more than the loving, sincere longing and yearning to unite with your fellow humans and with God. This is what the entire Universe is about.

W: I know this sounds crazy, Emmanuel, but I find myself thinking of you as my best and dearest friend.

E: Thank you, and I tell you it's not crazy at all, for there have been times as I have said, when we have been together, and we shall be in the future.

W: Have we ever been involved before, Emmanuel, in some kind of teaching and serving as we are now?

E: Not in the way that you are envisioning and that would please you most. I'm sorry, my friend. But most certainly in our mutuality as we exist now and have existed in past lives when you were physical and I was not, there has been much that has been done in that area, which most certainly is now on the threshold of expansion.

W: How is it, Emmanuel, that as a Soul, as a Consciousness, you as well as the other Spirits around me seem to be always either male or female? Isn't a Soul both male and female? Isn't a Soul androgynous?

< 80 >

E: Absolutely, but so long as you are involved in the duality of male and female, there tends to be identification with either one aspect or the other. And so long as you remain in the dualistic state, Spirits most likely will be perceived as being masculine or feminine, according to their connection to you, what aspect of yourself and what aspect of them is manifested in your life at that moment. In other words, we are all androgynous, you as well. And yet it is such a difficult thing to accept that unification in your physical world, because you do live in a state of either/or illusion. But there is a call, a need now to stand forth in a deeper state of unity. Things are becoming more closely aligned, as you know, and many people are accepting their androgynous natures.

Some are expressing it in homosexuality, which is a distortion, to be sure, but one which nevertheless in the long run can perhaps be a very healthy statement. And I do indeed say that homosexuality, whether it be male or female, is a distortion, for there is still the need in your civilization to accept the sexual structure of the physical reality in which you exist. But of and by itself homosexuality is an indication of a rising awareness that in time will come to truth, where each person will be able to accept both aspects of themselves, the assertive and the receptive, the masculine and the feminine, and neither will have an onus attached to it, nor will there be a sense of better or worse.

W: I have another question about past lives, Emmanuel, and it has to do with Jesus. Several times lately I have found myself saying to my students, "That's not

< 81 >

what Jesus was teaching," or "He didn't say that," probably referring to some quotation in the Bible, and when somebody would ask me how I knew, I would find myself replying, "Because I was there," which of course sounds totally outrageous. But you know, Emmanuel, there are times when I feel as though I really was there.

E: The sensing of the presence of Christ is essential to you, dear friend, for in the teachings that are coming through you, that are beginning to penetrate through you, there is an element of His intent, and whether you wish to claim your presence there or His presence here is completely up to you.

Indeed, the deep and profound experience of the wisdom of that Entity, that lifted Being which you are becoming aware of, is an experience that is truly available to everyone in human form.

All that is required is to ask, but there is such tenderness in all of you dear humans that is locked so and guarded so and defended against so inside the heart of each one of you, there is such shyness and reluctance even to whisper your need. If you could help those who come to you, dear Wingate, to open their hearts as you have done to their own deep and eternal longing and encourage them to utter that need, it would be one of the most important gifts you could give.

W: But what will I say, Emmanuel? Where will the words come from?

E: From you heart, dear Wingate. From your heart. You are a holy man, and in that reality whatever comes into your own heart is what you should say.

< 82 >

W: That's a pretty awesome responsibility, Emmanuel.

E: It is, but it is also an opportunity to open to your own leadership.

W: So then at one level it will be *my* words, *my* guidance, but then at another level the words will be coming through me as me, and then at still another level there won't be any me at all, just us—but unfortunately I haven't gotten to that delightful space yet. I still have some growing to do. Where you are you're still growing too, aren't you, Emmanuel?

E: Indeed.

W: But there's no doubt or guilt at your level, is there?

E: Fortunately, that has been dissolved and transformed. I am growing in my ability to conceive of the true meaning of God and the true meaning of creativity and of eternal expansion, and so I no longer need to burden myself with guilt, for I no longer believe that there is one molecule of my Consciousness that is separate from His.

W: You say that the ultimate step that each Soul has to take is to totally surrender to the Will of God. Have you taken that step, Emmanuel?

E: I have.

W: Of course, because I think you went on to say that once a Soul has taken that step, then It's finished with

< 83 >

this School and It can move on to another one where there's no more guilt and doubt and all of the other things that It has been struggling with.

E: Exactly. And while you have experienced such times in your own Consciousness when all the shackles fell away and you sensed your Oneness and your eternal Reality, this is the way that I have learned to exist.

W: In other words, you are in that space all the time that I'm in just for a moment now and then. It must be total bliss, Emmanuel.

E: Indeed it is, my friend. Indeed it is. You'll see.

< 84 >

DIALOGUE FOURTEEN

17 July 1980

E: It gives me such pleasure and joy to see you again in this mode, my dear friend, for though we speak often through the day, you and I, there are seldom times of such concentrated communication as transpires here in this room, so rather than have you perceive me at some higher level of Consciousness, I thought I would join you in a mutuality this morning, if I may, by sitting here on your left. For I exist as you exist and we are essentially One, are we not? So don't look for me up there. Look for me here, sitting next to you and holding your hand, as I often yearn to do. It must be allowed, this intimacy between our levels of Consciousness. It is essential. It is essential.

And now, dear Wingate, to the matters at hand. There are things that are troubling you.

W: Yes, there are, Emmanuel, and one of them is what to do about *Tilling the Soul*. No publisher is knocking my door down, and it's very hard for me just to sit and do nothing.

< 85 >

E: To be doing something is, of course, far easier than to be doing what seems to be nothing, yet there are many times, as you know, when doing nothing can be far more productive. And through the trust that you have so wondrously found within you in your past experiences you have come to the realization that the wisdom of the Soul, if allowed to function unencumbered, will bring about the desired results. There is no need to be concerned yet, or of course at all, about the publication of your work, but the time is not yet right for you to take a hand.

Now I do not mean to sound mysterious, or in any way assume a cloak-and-dagger attitude, but it is the Soul's process that is the purpose of Life and not the writing or the publishing of a book, and it is therefore the Soul's process to which I address myself. It is the letting go of the conscious will and the assuming of the authority of the Higher Will. It is the yielding, it is the simply letting go, trusting your Intuition and not your conscious mind to guide you, knowing that when it is the proper time you will be presented with the wisdom you require, whether you are sitting here in this room or somewhere else. All is well, my friend, all is well. How else can I say this to you? All of your efforts are not shelved indefinitely but are simply awaiting their proper time.

W: What do you think of including some of the things you have said to me in our dialogues together?

E: No, no, it's your book.

W: Our book, Emmanuel. Remember, we are partners.

< 86 >

E: Very well, dear Wingate, our book, but it is not through me that you are illuminated, but through you that I am illuminated. And when I say "I," I speak editorially for all of us who are involved, as you and I are now, in the process of the education of the world. Perhaps I should educate you, my friend, as to the value of what you have created, for you tend to see it in modest terms rather than as a key that can be an essential element of growth for many, many people. Think for a moment, if you will, of a city adrift upon a sea of confusion, of need and of fear that so many of your fellow humans are now experiencing, and then think of them being given the guiding light of a presentation such as yours. My dear friend, how can you help but realize the extreme value of what you have done? And yet here you are finding it so difficult to acknowledge the light and the wisdom within you. Indeed, you seem to find it far easier and more comfortable to give them over to someone else rather than to claim them as your own. And you must begin to claim them as your own, my friend. You must.

W: It will be a lot easier if I can just hold on to the feeling of the editorial "I." What a wonderful way to express the perfect union, the total Oneness. "We" and "our" always gave me such a good feeling of partnership and togetherness, and of course they still do, but now I see how they also carry within them a sense of separation. There can't be a "we" without there first also being a "me" and a "thee." But then in those moments when I am in that place in me and you are in that place in you where we are really One, then there is no more "we," is there, but only "I"?

< 87 >

And yet even in our mutuality we still need to use those words of ultimate separation, and so, dear Emmanuel, if "we" have time I do have one more matter at hand to talk about. Remember the last time I was here how you spoke briefly on homosexuality? Well, in the months since then two gay students have started studying with me, and I don't know all that much about homosexuals, but they're Souls, too, and have the same spiritual needs as the rest of us, don't they?

E: Of course, there is no question that they, like you, are involved in the process of growth, and just because they have chosen, many of them only because it seems to be fashionable, to claim themselves as deviant to the natural physical process of reproduction does not in any way separate them, as many of them hope it does, from the rest of humanity. Indeed, many of them are not essentially gay, but have found themselves lonely, have found themselves needing to belong, have found themselves swept along by the sudden notoriety and acclaim of that kind of orientation, and so it is best, as you have suggested, to ignore the differences and to focus on the oneness, the sameness.

Talk to them as a friend, but also assume the role of the parent, which is a portion of your being, and guide them not to ignore their confusions or their needs, for of course each Soul has clothed Itself in this particular life with what that Soul needs to grow through in order to be transformed, but not to become hypnotized by them either. Their sexuality is a very small part of who they really are. It is simply one aspect of the Soul's desire to find expression, and where there is difficulty then they must be helped to understand that somewhere they are

< 88 >

not hearing the voice of truth, for if they were indeed in truth there would not be the great array of difficulties they seem to experience in interpersonal relationships.

In a meditation such as yours truth can be found, and that truth will bring them peace and fulfillment, even though this may require that they put down the mask that they have so recently put on and discover their true identity, and this, of and by itself, takes extreme courage. For those who have struggled to find their inner truth and have found that their truth is homosexuality, I have nothing but respect and admiration. For those who are not in the struggle in honesty but are simply aligning themselves with something that is not their truth, I must urge them to find their truth before they claim their allegiance.

W: The things that you say are so meaningful, Emmanuel, and I wonder if it would be all right for me to start sharing you with those who come to study with me?

E: It is entirely up to you, my dear friend. If you feel there is wisdom in what I have been privileged to present, then by all means share it. We did not come together just to bring you through a crisis, you know. We came together because there is work to be done, but I again urge you to trust your own Intuition, your own wisdom, whatever is truth to you. For it is your truth that you are sharing as well as mine. It is important that you realize this, for there is no way that something I say would appear to be truth to you if you did not already know it. It would sound far too alien for you to accept, and you quite rightly would challenge it, or at least shelve it until some future time.

< 89 >

Whatever adheres to the heart as truth adheres because there is a voice within the heart that has called the truth to it.

My truth is your truth, as your truth is my truth, and this is another way we come together, how the oneness can be experienced. And as we share this truth with others, there is then a widening of the circle. If there are some within your classroom who do not adhere to that truth, it does not mean that they do not belong there. It means that somewhere there is another voice that they are hearing, and that other voice needs to be discovered and brought forth. It may be the voice of their own uniqueness and of another path, or it may be the voice of confusion and denial, and that is where you then can help them. Again, it is a matter of trusting, trusting, always trusting. And how can one trust God and the universe if one cannot trust one's own Intuition?

You know, my dear Wingate, if I thought you would accept it I would design a costume for you to be worn in Spirit, something to elevate you in your self-esteem so that you could begin to feel that it is your own wisdom that you share with others. But then you would soon tire of it and throw it off as giving you more grandeur than you are comfortable with.

W: Perhaps I could handle an image of myself from time to time in a simple monk's robe, Emmanuel, but anything more than that, even in Spirit, would seem as though I was setting myself up as some kind of self-proclaimed Master, and I don't want that. I want my students to have a sense of Oneness and partnership with me, as I do with you.

< 90 >

E: Of course, my friend, and there is no reason why this should not be, but along with the reality of Universal Oneness there is also a duality that exists in the physical world, and in that duality there is no question that you are a Teacher of Truth, that you are indeed a Master, and though I am not in any way pushing a costume upon you, it is this duality that I am urging you to become more comfortable with.

W: I really don't feel worthy of being called a Master, Emmanuel.

E: I know, my friend, I know, but what do you think being a Master consists of, and what do you think it requires of you, and how do you believe it should manifest? Does a Master attract a great number of followers? Not necessarily. Or have a large ashram or become a guru? Very seldom, most often not. A Master, in my vocabulary, is quite simply one who has resolved the enigma of human existence, who understands its purpose, and who is willing to witness to that understanding.

W: And that's it, Emmanuel? And whether or not others are drawn to the understanding doesn't matter?

E: Not all, my friend, not at all. A Master's task is not to transform another but simply to be available.

W: Thank you, Emmanuel, and bless you. You've made it so much easier for me to be comfortable with this new image of myself. But it's still going to take time to be able to accept it completely, you must know that.

< 91 >

E: To be able to walk with the gentle pride of a Master and the open heart of a sage? Of course, my dear friend, but your willingness to follow my guidance in this as in all of our communications is truly a wondrous gift you give me, and I want you to know that I deeply appreciate it.

< 92 >

DIALOGUE FIFTEEN

20 December 1980

W: I seem to be stuck on one of those plateaus again, Emmanuel, or maybe it's the same one, and I know there's so much more ahead of me and I can't help but want to start growing again.

E: All in due time, my friend, all in due time. You want to take your place in a much broader scheme of things, I know, and your awareness, your curiosity, your questions, your need to understand reach very far out indeed. But the effect of expanded growth, of accelerated Consciousness, can at times take one very quickly to limitation, which seems to belie the very nature of expansion. And yet it does not, for there are realities in the human consciousness that carry with them limitations quite necessary to the humanness involved, and therein lies another deeply important aspect of the learning process. You cannot be all that you know yourself to be while you are still human. Does that sound like a contradiction?

< 93 >

W: Yes, it does, Emmanuel.

E: Yet it is not, dear Wingate, for as you approach the doorway to Spiritual knowing you also feel more and more the constriction of the human bondage, the human vessel. As the Consciousness expands and expands, as the awareness grows and grows, as the capabilities become more and more manifest, there is always a pointed silhouette of the human imperfection, but this is not something to be railed against or to be fought or to be denied. Rather, it is to be understood and accepted.

W: So then we can realize that something is true but we can't experience it as being true while we are still in human form.

E: Exactly. Now I am not in any way suggesting that there are not still areas within you that can be expanded and experienced, not at all, not at all, but there are limits to the human capability to understand, and it is fruitless for you to demand that you go beyond these limitations.

W: But what about Christ Consciousness, Emmanuel, or Buddha Consciousness? I, we, all of us can look forward to going that far, can't we?

E: It would seem so, my friend, wouldn't it, yet how does one truly know without the personal reality of it what was experienced by Christ, or by Buddha, or by any of the other evolved Souls that have from time to time touched upon the earth? How does one know the

< 94 >

true nature of their Being, whether they were of humanness or whether they were of God? These things are much more in the realm of the expanded Consciousness than they are in the realm of human consciousness.

When you spoke of the Consciousness of Christ and of Buddha, we were speaking of Them as human beings, much as you are a human being, and yet I must say to you that there is a difference. For if it were not possible that someone of a higher wisdom could enter into human form, what then would you have to look forward to when you are finished with your reincarnational cycles? And if a greater Consciousness than what you are aware of now could not exist, what then would be the purpose of the careful education and evolution of the individual Soul?

Of course there are wisdoms beyond yours, and this was my initial intent as we began to speak, to say to you that it is not all here, it is not all available here in your physical world, there is more, much more, to which you are all heir and to which you will move in the reasonable pace of your own capacity and willingness to grow.

W: But who would want it any other way, Emmanuel, who would want their education to stop once they had their master's degree in what I think of as Christ Consciousness, or perhaps I should say Jesus Consciousness, from school Planet Earth? And haven't you always said that the last and ultimate lesson that we have to learn here in this school before we graduate is the total acceptance of the Will of God manifest in an

< 95 >

open heart, and isn't that what the life of Jesus was all about?

E: So then when you speak of Christ Consciousness you are speaking of the aspects of the man Jesus who yielded to the Will of God.

W: Yes, yes. That and all the other things that seem to go with that elevated level of Consciousness, like unconditional love and joy and a sense of total Oneness with all things. Like the kind of Consciousness that you have, Emmanuel. And I think of Buddha Consciousness, as well as Cosmic Consciousness and what I call Soul Consciousness, as having very much the same aspects of Christ Consciousness.

E: It seems as though we speak of weighty matters, you and I, and that is part of the pleasurable interchange that I enjoy so much with you.

W: And I with you, my dear friend and Teacher.

E: We have been through quite a few things together, have we not, in the past as well as in this life. I cannot tell you how pleasant it has been, and will continue to be, to find you again in this physical form and to have you, through much guidance—which would be perceived as manipulation, perhaps, in your human form, if it were not to the good intent of our coming again together—weave your way to this place and this time, for I longed to speak to you again.

W: Have you always been my Teacher, in the past as well as now, Emmanuel?

< 96 >

E: Not quite so, no. There were times when we were physical companions and we learned from each other, and in that I was no more a Teacher than you. But we have now moved into perhaps a more clearly discernible posture of student and Teacher, and yet I yearn not to have that distinction too clearly delineated. One learns when one is willing to learn, from whatever teaching device is at hand, and had I not been able to contact you, most certainly, and you are well aware of this, the learning would still have taken place. When the Soul is ready, whatever it yearns to know is available, for the entire Universe is rich in the lore that will bring the wisdom to it. It is all there, yes, even in the very rocks and trees that cover your earth there is wisdom.

W: You know, Emmanuel, I think part of the impatience that I was talking about earlier comes from my being bogged down in so much endless detail that really doesn't seem to be important. Some of it is necessary, I know, like feeding and caring for my physical body and paying the rent, but at least they help to keep me grounded, and yet I can't help but wonder if a lot of this isn't just getting in the way of my next step, which I have a feeling is going to be a big one.

E: What is being sensed here with some validity is that the next step, which in all probability will be the last and final step of acquiescence to the Higher Will, involves the relinquishing of not only what may seem to you to be necessities and allowing yourself to become, and perhaps I speak idealistically now, simply the ear to hear and the eye to see, without the accumulated sense of need for balance and anchoring, which at this point

< 97 >

in the Soul's development is becoming a limitation. And this does not mean that when you relinquish form you will cease to eat or physically function. Not at all, but there will be a different aspect to the requirement. Now instead of serving the purpose of anchoring it will simply be something that will be attended to without effort in the new expanded state of Consciousness. And it does not mean that because one yields to a free flow one will be structureless, but rather that one's life will take on an organic structure or, perhaps even more correctly, that the structure that is there will lose its rigidity and become a new kind of structureless structure that is a part of the expanded state.

W: So then all that has to change is our Consciousness and our awareness.

E: And the fear, which is a reality in every human being, of structurelessness, the fear that one does not have a cosmic inner structure, which of course everyone does.

W: It seems like it's a time for me to be quiet, Emmanuel, and give this new expandedness you speak of a chance to germinate.

E: Which will be a time of most active and intense inner activity, dear friend, not ruled or directed by the mind at all, much as your deep meditation is a most active and vitally alive and creative time and yet to all outer appearances you have assumed a state of almost nonhuman passivity. As you enter this state of receptivity and, as you say, of germination, which is an

< 98 >

excellent, excellent word, I envision a brilliant light that is focused in the center of your Being and is nourishing itself through the rays of every hue that is discernible to you and many that are not, from the deepest purple up to the most brilliant gold, and you are all-encompassed by these wonderful rays of nurturing Consciousness. And so, when there is the sense, by those who look and often judge, that you have retired from active physical participation, I cannot but smile at the distortion that exists in that judgment.

W: If you will forgive me, Emmanuel, I know how you dislike dealing with time, but how long do you see me in this period of germination?

E: Why, until the natural inclination to begin the movement outward again is evident. But the period of germination will not be a time of imprisonment or of rigidity. There will be times when the germination will be paramount, and times when it will be a deeper reality and other things will be paramount, but once you have entered into it the germination will be a more or less constant state. Even I in my seemingly elevated Consciousness have been maintaining a state within myself that would be termed much the same as the one we are speaking of for you, where there is always the Self, the God within each Consciousness that must always be in a state of awareness of Its own germination. This is the true creativity.

And so as you nurture your human consciousness from the wealth and richness that you are amassing in that portion of you that is in a state of germination, you will never want to cease that germination, but will take

< 99 >

from it and then move outward and then go back and take from it and then move outward again. So in terms of day-to-day activity, although it will be a time of quiet and of conscious inner growth, there will also be within that time periods of intense outer activity, for the moment that you touch the element of vital creation within, you will have to express it outwardly. This will become your way of existing, and there will be a groundedness there and a structure that is both Cosmic and organic, and yet, oddly enough, this is a state that the human being is reluctant to enter into, holding on instead to structures that seem to be so necessary but are really only handrails. And so, not to digress from your question of how long you will be in this state of germination, I had to explain all of these things before I could give you the answer, *eternally.*

W: We do speak of weighty matters, don't we, Emmanuel, but if you will bear with me, as you always so graciously do, there is one more thing that I would like to go over with you, and that is the prickly subject of Will and Surrender and Free Will and Choice, because some of the things you say and my own truths and realizations don't seem to be always in agreement, and I'd like to go over them with you to see if indeed there are any differences, or if it isn't, as I suspect, simply our words getting in the way of our understanding.

For example, I feel that with Soul Consciousness there is the realization that there is an Unfolding Plan, that there is a Will that is the dynamic energy behind this Plan, that this Will is how God expresses Itself and that Surrender is how God experiences Itself, and that it is through our will that we express the Unfolding Plan

< 100 >

and it is through our surrender that we experience It. I also feel that the will to flow with the Plan, to help bring It into being, is the only will we ever need to have, and that opening to the Plan and accepting It is the only surrender we ever need to make, and that with this flowing acceptance, this perfect blending of will and surrender, there is no longer any need for Free Will, which is so full of doubt and anxiety and guilt, that we are now filled with only the One Will perfectly express- ing itself in us and through us. Which seems very much in harmony with what you said about no longer needing to burden yourself with guilt because you no longer believed that there was one molecule of your Conscious- ness that was separate from God. But then you also said at another time that you have Free Will.

E: Ah, but see, my dear friend, here is where verbal- ization has perhaps broken down. For when I speak of Free Will I am not speaking of the narrow egocentric will that exists in the distorted aspect of each Soul, the part of the human consciousness that says my will, my way, my plan, and which is the portion of the human consciousness that has come to be transformed. I am speaking rather of the Free Will that chooses to know God's Will. That is the fundamental use of Free Will, and it is only from this deeper level of understanding that the act of surrender can be made.

One cannot say from one's ego consciousness that one surrenders to the Will of God. This can be said a thousand times a day, and yet because it is said with the human consciousness to gain something from that surrender, there is guilt and all of the other manifesta- tions that are so unpleasant in the human experience.

< 101 >

But when one can let go of the distorted need for controlling and for specialness and for all of the other aspects of defense that go to make up the prison of each human being's existence, then one can find within oneself the true Desire, and the Free Will that is so much spoken of can be seen in its natural state, which is the choice to surrender to the Will of God.

This is the ultimate use of Free Will, which is, of course, much, much different from the will that likes to posture as the expanded Free Will but is only the will of the child, speaking in a voice that would like to be heard as the Free Will of Higher Consciousness but nevertheless is not that at all, and so when we speak of Free Will it must be made clear which will is being spoken of.

W: But isn't it always the One Will in us that Willeth? And Chooseth? And isn't all Free Will but a lower vibration of the One Will, perfectly expressing Itself in us and through us?

E: Absolutely.

W: And so instead of growing through Free Will and Choice, then, we grow through experience.

E: But you choose to have the experience.

W: Do you still choose, Emmanuel?

E: Oh yes, indeed. I choose to serve. I choose to be with you at this moment. All in accordance with the Divine Plan.

< 102 >

W: All in accordance with the Divine Plan. So then it's a matter of Consciousness, isn't it, Emmanuel? At one level there is the kind of Will that chooses only to follow the Divine Plan, and then at a lower level there is the other kind of will. But if there is an Unfolding Plan, if in the beginning there was a First Cause, or a First Choice, if you will, then everything that has happened since or ever will happen must be the result of that First Cause, and so it seems to me that even God does not have the Free Will or the Free Choice to change the Plan, and so the whole concept of Free Will and Free Choice seems to me to be only a necessary but temporary illusion.

E: Absolutely. Of course this is true. For is not your physical reality an illusion, and so of course all things that relate to it are illusion also? What you are speaking of now, dear friend, is a state of Grace, where all things regardless of their Consciousness are One with God.

We are speaking here of many levels of reality, many levels of awareness, where in the totalness there is but One, but within that One there are countless Consciousnesses that are seeking their own identity, and one cannot become aware of one's own Consciousness without the actual act of choosing.

You would prefer at some level to be a fatalist and to say that it was meant to be. And of course ultimately you are meant to be who you in your essence are, but to say that it does not matter what you choose, it will all happen anyway, is wrong, because then you are abdicating the portion of you that is God.

< 103 >

W: But when I speak of a Plan and our being partners in Its unfolding, Emmanuel, I also think of us as partners in Its creation, as co-creators, and if that's fatalism then I don't mind, because it's not the negative kind where it's all going to happen anyway so why bother to even get up in the morning, which may or may not be part of the Plan. Instead I feel that we're all helping to fulfill what I think of as "Our" Plan, which seems to me to be a very positive and creative thing to be doing.

And if there is no First Cause and no Unfolding Plan, or if there is a Plan and we can all decide how we want to modify It, then it seems to me that we have a Chaos, an anarchy, like trying to build the Empire State Building without an architect and with everyone running around doing their thing, instead of an ordered Universe, a Cosmos, with a Plan and a structure which we have all had a hand in designing and which we are now in the process of bringing into being.

E: But there is a stability in the Cosmos, dear friend, that allows for the Chaos of individual decision-making. Be aware of that. And I must disagree with the concept that if Souls were allowed to choose they would run helter-skelter and there would be very little organized movement back toward the Oneness. Each Soul in Its essence, in Its Godliness, is yearning toward the Light, and to have faith in that, regardless of what that Soul in Its ignorance chooses to do along the way, is perhaps the key. For if each Soul is allowed to go in whatever Free Will way It chooses to, It will ultimately choose to go back to God, and therein lies the fundamental structure.

< 104 >

All is well, dear friend, and the Universe is ordered and benign. And yet in that Universe there is certainly room for each person's errors and confusions, for the Universe is vast and flowing, and it does not take offense or issue with negativity but simply allows it, knowing full well that in the natural balance and flow the negativity will be transformed into light again. And it is only through the issuance of the license for choice, if we may use that unfortunate word one more time, that this can take place. For in the act of love there is no forcing. In the moment of Truth one cannot be forced, but each Soul must comply willingly from the depth of Its open heart.

W: Which means that the part of God that is in us as us has Free Will and Choice also. But can God be arbitrary? Can God change Its Mind? Can God change Its Plan? What about the First Cause? Wasn't It perfect, whole and unchangeable?

E: Absolutely. Let me go further with this, dear Wingate. One changes and alters, regardless of the extent of one's freedom, only so long as one remains to some degree separated from Oneness. Once Oneness becomes a thing of reality then one enters into Beingness, and when one is in a state of Beingness then what is one to change, and what is one to alter, and what is one to strive against? For all things at that moment simply are.

Rest with this, my dear friend, rest with this, and if it cannot be understood by the conscious mind then switch to your Intuition and let whatever is still not perceived rest there, and in time the greater Mind, the Mind of the Soul, will give a sense of knowing that goes far beyond the vocabulary of knowing.

< 105 >

DIALOGUE SIXTEEN

18 June 1981

E: It is as though there is a glass between us, my dear Wingate, a window made of the subtlest material, so subtle that there are times when you are not even aware of its existence, yet it separates us nevertheless, and it is time to open it up. Now I am not speaking of opening your channel, but rather I am suggesting that although there is the deepest knowledge of Truth, of Divinity, of Light, of God by whatever title you wish to call It, in your Consciousness, in the Essence of you, there is still a slight sense of removal, as though you cannot yet quite claim your place in the universal scheme as one of us, and this is something that I wish to address, for it is no longer necessary for you to remain even slightly out of the center of things.

You have always been in our hearts, my dear friend, and it is now time to be in our hands—in our arms, as it were—even though you are still in a physical body. You have striven so long and so well since the moment of conception within your Higher Consciousness of the yearning to return to the womb, to your Oneness with God, and it is just one more step, one more step, and it

< 106 >

is not even a step of willingness. *Willingness*, that is a
strange word to use with you, is it not, for in your
Higher Consciousness you are totally willing, and yet
there is a residual withholding, there is the questioning,
there is the doubt that is part of the human baggage that
no longer has validity to you but is there perhaps only
out of habit.

But even though the window is there, dear Wingate,
it can be worked around, you know. It can be gone over
or through. It need not be completely erased. Choose to
believe, even though there is a sense of unsureness;
choose to accept, even though what you sense will in all
probability be familiar to you. Indeed, there is a reason-
ableness to familiarity, for if something were totally
foreign, if familiarity were totally absent, then there
would be no way of relating to what you perceive. This
does not mean that the Expanded Consciousness cannot
manifest Itself. Not at all. It simply means that It must
manifest Itself in accordance with Its perception of Its
own humanness. And yet this manifestation will not be
illusion, it will not be falsity, it will simply be the focus
that is available to you at this time in the Soul's growth.
Most certainly you will be far more able to perceive
without your human body—this is without question, of
course—but in the meantime here you are in a human
body, one that you have chosen, one that you have
struggled with mightily, one that has served you ex-
ceedingly well.

Fear no longer that in your desire to see and to hear
and to experience you will become the means of self-
trickery. This cannot be. If there is a slight bending to
one's own pleasure, well, what of that? Are you not
creator of your own world? How many times have we

< 107 >

said this? And if you create an image of God that is very much like your own, why, this is not so far wrong, is it, for you and God most certainly are One. There is a need to go beyond your human incapacity to see and your human doubts to the reality of your Consciousness as it is now expanding into my world, so that you and I can speak as one. There is no reason why this cannot happen, except for the residual effects of that glass, that symbolic separation that we have been talking about.

W: I'm beginning to wish I could somehow break that glass, Emmanuel.

E: Such an extreme action is not at all necessary, as I have already pointed out to you. Instead, may I suggest that while you are sitting in meditation you construct in your imagination a vision of how you would like to perceive my being to your own satisfaction, and I care very little how I am conceived so long as it is positive. This is not a false way but a very useful way for you to begin to dissolve that remaining separation.

W: Could you give me a few hints, Emmanuel? I think it would help me if you would.

E: Gladly, dear Wingate. To begin with, I am lighted. I am a golden light with a great amount of white intermingled, and as I am perceived I am perhaps six feet five or so, and of proportionate dimension. I am of masculine countenance, though the difficulty, the effect of putting in too close a definition of my features could become distracting, and so blur the lens of your inner conscious eye; see me as a light forming more or less

< 108 >

the image of a man. Then allow yourself to accept the image as truth, and I assure you that there will be much truth there, though it will not be perfection, but close enough, and the time between your perception of me in your imagination and the time when you are able to accept that image, with some slight alteration perhaps, as the reality of my presence will be very short indeed.

Be aware, however, that in the initial connection there will be a great focusing, indeed, a demand that you will place upon the image, the Light. There will be strain. The moment that you sense this, and you will sense it in the physical nature as well as the emotional nature, allow yourself to relax and allow the Light to move farther and farther away without losing contact with it. Fear not, I will remain, the Light will remain. And then as you yield to the reality of that Light, as you allow yourself to become open to it, there will be a sense of connecting deep within that will give you the courage, that will give you the faith in the validity of your imaging and allow you to move to the deeper state of receptivity where I will speak to you.

Again, it is not a matter of forcing or self-discipline. This goes far beyond that. It is a matter of accepting what already exists within you, it is a matter of allowing for what in reality already is. And that symbolic glass is not your enemy, my dear friend. It is something that has been vitally necessary to you, not only in this life but for many, many lives, going back to the time when you first became aware of Spirit and of Higher Consciousness, and it must not be carelessly tossed away or deeply criticized. It has a usefulness in your world, and will continue to have until such a point of expansion is reached that there is no longer any desire to remain

< 109 >

separate from the total Reality as you are able to perceive it in human form.

In the meantime be content to know, dear Wingate, that though the glass remains in a portion of your Consciousness intact and functioning, there is a broader portion of your Consciousness that is now able to step over it, as it were, or to go through it, to function as though it did not exist. This will become more and more intense, more believable, more real and more expanded, and as time goes on the glass, not with the necessity of being smashed but simply with the working around it and accepting its reality but not its validity, will slowly dissolve. And I urge you to put aside all thought of when it will happen and simply know that it is part of the Plan. No strident moves are necessary. Only the realization that yes, of course it is there, for are you not human? But you also know that there is a reality beyond this glass, that there is a way for you to connect deeply and profoundly with that Reality, and that you can do that by the means that are available to you without in any way criticizing or shattering the glass that has been so essential to you and that has allowed you to see so many, many things. Indeed, the glass used to be a very thick wall that was completely impenetrable, but it has been worn thin, eroded by the struggle and the commitment of your Soul through many, many incarnations. You have no idea the patience, the fortitude, the courage, the love, that It has had to encompass in Its being in order to move through these lifetimes.

W: I really didn't mean what I said about breaking the glass, Emmanuel. I was just feeling a little frustrated, I guess, at the thought of its being there between us. I

< 110 >

like the meditation you have suggested much better. I know it's going to work for me, and I wonder if it's not something I might also share with others who are striving to connect with *their* Emmanuel.

E: This most certainly is not a secret communication, and it will be a pleasure for you to share it, I am sure, at some future time. But for now, at least until you feel more secure with it, let us keep it in the family.

W: Let's hope it won't take too long, Emmanuel, and meanwhile one thing puzzles me about the way you describe yourself, and that is why you are only of a masculine nature. Souls are both male and female, aren't they?

E: Of course, my friend, of course, but my communication is of a masculine nature in that it is the active principle of teaching, and I am therefore more comfortable in a masculine countenance. However, there are also times of nurturing as well as when a deep healing is taking place, and you will then be aware of a more feminine vibration. Most certainly you in your humanness are aware, as you have already stated, that you yourself have both masculine and feminine aspects, as does every human being, and there are moments of receptivity when you choose to identify with the feminine, and yet there are many more times when you identify with the masculine. This can be confusing in matters of life adjustment and what is expected and so on and so forth, but there will come a time, and we are all striving for this, and it is indeed already evident in your world, when one will not be forced, if you will,

< 111 >

THE BOOK OF SURRENDER

into one role or another, but will have complete allowance of choice. Not in a physical sense, I wish to make this clear, for there is a great necessity in the learning process to be either masculine or feminine, for both have very different roles and very different lessons, but in the Consciousness sense, and this will be a most blessed time indeed.

W: Another thing, Emmanuel, you didn't mention having chakras or centers of Consciousness when you described yourself, just the gold-and-white light. Does this mean that where you are you don't need them anymore?

E: Only as a means of communication between my world and yours, where the concept of the division of Consciousness is a very useful and indeed a Divinely directed one. But also know within you as a Master that they are in the greater reality an illusion and are simply witnessing to the possibility of the greater Self, the True Self that is within each one of you. And yet until the Consciousness is freed of the illusion of separation and there is therefore no longer the need for differentiation of any kind, the various chakras as you are aware of them will continue to serve an important function.

W: I really look forward to graduating from this school that I've been going to for so many lifetimes, Emmanuel, even though I know there are other schools with other lessons to be learned and other challenges to face. Does it ever stop?

E: My dear friend, challenge exists through eternity.

W: I'm sure it does, and I'm so glad.

E: Of course you are, and aren't we all? If there were no more challenges than we would stop creating, and what a dismal state that would be, for only in the challenge and the creativity that comes from the challenge can we experience the many facets of Self.

W: Yes, and what a wonderful thing it is, Emmanuel, to have you spell out what I can do to dissolve or get around that glass that is still between us, even to the point of describing what you look like.

E: I speak to you now in a somewhat human image, but when you decide to leave your physical body I will appear to be of an even larger dimension.

W: Will I still be able to recognize you, Emmanuel? I mean, there will be a lot of other Souls around too, won't there?

E: Of course you will, my dear friend, but do not be concerned; we will discuss this much more before the time actually comes.

< 113 >

DIALOGUE SEVENTEEN

28 November 1981

W: That glass that we spoke of in our last dialogue still seems to be there, dear Emmanuel, and I wonder if there isn't something more I could be doing to get rid of it besides visualizing you and then blurring the lens and relaxing and allowing your image of you to move farther and farther away from me, as you suggested I do.

E: My dear friend, the closer one moves to Oneness the more one needs to move away from even the desire for Oneness, or more particularly the striving toward Oneness, for the striving can work rather to oppose the Oneness than to encompass It or to serve It. And so the time has come when you must put aside the yearning and hoping and striving and be willing simply to accept what exists, for you see, my dear Wingate, we will come together in communion and communication not because of your striving or desire or of my dearest wishes, but simply because we both exist. You exist and I exist, for you, with you, and all about you.

Hold the image before you of a slowly opening and unfolding flower. There is no need to wonder "Will that

< 114 >

flower unfold?"; of course it will, that is its truth, its nature. Trust, then, that your nature is unfolding as it is meant to unfold, not as it is taught or educated or forced to unfold or willed to unfold, and that in the process of your Soul's evolution through eons of seeking you have come to this plateau. It is yours, it is your home, and you belong here, every bit as much as I do.

And therefore when you question the delay or what you must do in addition to what you are already doing, my answer must be that there is nothing to be done but to accept this Reality, to acknowledge your citizenship in It, as it were, and simply to allow It to unfold. I do not say this to frustrate you, my dear friend, but only to assure you that all that needs to be done is being done, all that is required is being met, and now must come the unfolding and the accepting of the total reality of our companionship.

W: Sometime I can do that in my meditation, Emmanuel, and then the feeling I have is so strong that there's no question but that you are with me. And then there are other times when I'm not sure at all.

E: I'm always there with you, my dear Wingate, I'm always there. Never question it.

W: It feels as though you're beside me, Emmanuel— not right beside me but a little in front of me, where we can see each other easily, but not right in front of me either.

E: Exactly. In the manner of a country gentleman, I do not intrude upon your total vision, for there are things

< 115 >

that you are desirous and needful of receiving from others as well as from me. And besides, my companionship can be much better experienced in its true reality, as I long for you to experience it, if I sit at your side in comradeship, rather than sit before you as a removed or too highly elevated Being.

Again, there is no need for stress or strain, but when there is, I urge you not to hold whatever images or guidance you receive in question, for being human is not the easiest way to perceive total Truth. Indeed, it is quite difficult, so long as you are involved in the aspects of being human, to perceive even what is truly or strongly there, but there is never reason for questioning or doubt. This is the portion of your being that has come now fully to the focus, to the front of your awareness, and I, I am pleased to say, am serving as a catalyst in my association with you, and hopefully I will continue to be a catalyst throughout your life. Most certainly I pray that this will be so.

W: So do I, Emmanuel, so do I. I can't think of anything more wonderful. It feels so much better than the way you described yourself way back, as a go-between who would introduce me to other Souls and then pretty much disappear. Instead, you've become the most important part of that whole level of Consciousness for me, and I can't help but look forward to being with you when I no longer have my humanness to get in our way.

E: But don't you see, my friend, our communication became so rich and deep that there seemed to be no need to invite other Beings of Light, although those

< 116 >

who have chosen to serve and to work with you are most certainly available. Indeed, our focus together is of such a natural nature, it has such a warmth and flow and such a trust has been generated through our speaking together in this manner, that I would suggest that we continue to foster our more direct way of communicating.

And yes, I will be there, I and others you will know and recognize at the joyous moment when you have decided that you have had enough of this physical incarnation. It will be a lovely time of Light and reunion, and I look forward to it also.

W: Until that delightful moment all I want is to be a good partner in the work that we are doing together and serve in whatever way I can. At least I'm still in a physical body and so perhaps can do things that you and the others can't do. So use me, please use me, and let me know in no uncertain terms just what you want me to do.

E: Dear Wingate, whatever you have experienced, whoever you are as you perceive yourself to be, this is the most important thing that you have to offer. It is therefore not only what can be communicated through you, what you receive and give, but who you are yourself that can be of value to others, and in the full and clear representation of who you are, of your identity, of your feelings, of your experience, you have the greatest possible material for sharing, and the best possible guide as to how to do it. In other words, your work, in truth and alignment with your own inner being, is the greatest gift that you can give, and your

< 117 >

function in our work together is therefore to be who you are and to share that with your fellow humans.

So who are you, my dear friend, who are you? Every aspect of you has value. Share yourself freely, all of you, the humanness, the lightedness, the spiritual Teacher and the living breathing man, even the areas you hold slightly at a distance, all the things that you have experienced, all the things that you have learned from and grown from. Don't you see, my friend, they are treasures that you have to give, and simply because they might not all fit into your concept of spiritual Teaching you should not in any way eliminate them from your repertoire as you begin your work. Go with joy as the Being that you are, see others in the same Light, and share with them all of who you are and what you have experienced.

W: That would certainly include my having cancer, wouldn't it, and not just the specific steps that I took, but also the way I came to feel about it, becoming friendly with it, seeing it as a gift, things like that. For example, a man with cancer of the larynx came to see me yesterday, and even though I didn't feel he was ready to take the path you and I walked together, we talked for a couple of hours about the need to clean up his lake no matter what else he did and about the anger that had been burning in him for years, and I really think it helped.

E: My friend, you knew the nature of his problem, and in that you were most certainly helpful. Indeed, there are many, many more like him who are waiting to touch your hand in recognition of the similarity between your experience and theirs.

< 118 >

W: There is a very gifted healer who wants me to be her student, but only if I agree to work with her afterwards. And that doesn't feel right to me, Emmanuel. My work is supposed to be with you.

E: Without question. And yet, my friend, studying with someone can be helpful, for obvious reasons. For example, to offer a very simplistic illustration, if you had no knowledge of the anatomy of the human body and you wanted to place your hand in such a way that the energy would flow to a certain vital point, it would be less likely that you would administer the energy as effectively, again in an oversimplified illustration, as you would had you the knowledge of what the structure of the body was at that particular point.

In other words, there can be no information that if it is valid is not helpful. Always, of course, with the realization which we are all very clear about, and that is that guidance and Intuition take precedence over intellectual understanding.

W: You spoke last time of others in our group who would provide the feminine, nurturing aspect for our healing work, and I've had a strong feeling recently that one of them was, of all things, my own mother.

E: There is indeed a wondrous area of direct and complete knowing, available to all you dear humans, but you must first remove the barriers of expectation, which can be so subtle, so undetectable, that you could go through centuries of seeking and not even be aware of their existence. However, since we are now addressing each other clearly and directly, with very little if any

< 119 >

barrier left between us, I invite you to step beyond anything that you may expect to materialize, anything that you may expect to experience, and to join me in this area of infinite Light and Truth where there is no gentle place to sit and say "Ah yes, I have been here before, now I am quite safe." Of course you are safe, and yet there is the understandable reluctance to enter into a totally new Reality, and in this rather roundabout way I am addressing the question of your mother.

There has indeed been the emergence within you, as there will be within all in your world who are aware and willing to grow, of the need to recognize all aspects of the self both within and without, as the various Soul Consciousnesses choose to represent themselves. So does it not seem quite rational that since I have been represented to you quite fairly, I would say, as being of a masculine Consciousness in that I represent the active principle of teaching, is it not then reasonable that as you assume the role of a healer also there would be a longing and a desire for the nurturing feminine aspect as well? And what more logical form for the feminine to take than that of the most nurturing woman in your life, who was of course your mother. She does indeed exist on a level of understanding that would and does allow her to connect with you in your Higher Consciousness, but it is your opening to your own inner recesses that is allowing for this perception to take place. In this connection, it is of the utmost importance to maintain a state of balance between the masculine and feminine aspects, for if one is to be open and receptive to the Spirit forces of nurturing and sustaining, of caring—of the feminine, if you will—then without the masculine aspect one would simply sit in a pool of compassion and

< 120 >

cease to move forward and share that aspect with those who are in need of healing.

W: In our very first time together, Emmanuel, you said that I would attain Cosmic Consciousness in this lifetime, but another time you said something that suggested that I still had five more lessons to learn and that this might not be the end of my reincarnational cycles after all. And of course I much prefer the first scenario, but on the other hand if Unfolding is for me to come back to planet Earth and this school for Higher Consciousness for a few more lifetimes, then so be it.

E: I rather thought you would feel that way, dear Wingate. As you know, one can crowd much into one life or one can gently spread it about. It is not that there is a certain curriculum that is demanded of you. But as I reach into the elements of your Soul Consciousness I see the longing, the yearning to accomplish, to come to terms with, to understand—what words can I use, they are all so limited—to touch other awarenesses, to become a bit more than you are now. That is all, and this can most certainly be accomplished in very short order if you choose to do it in this way.

Try to envision, if you will, the Consciousness of Being, the Oneness with God that sought in the movement away from that Oneness not to deny or reject, but to seek out means of experiencing, of knowing in an individualized sense the Limitless Love and Light of Christ, of God, of Total Reality. It is in that seeking, my dear friend, that you have become who you are now, still seeking, I might add, new areas in which to recognize and to experience this wonderful Reality that

< 121 >

you have come to find, to reflect and to glorify in your own Being.

All I can say is that you are already vastly more than you imagine yourself to be, my very dear friend, even in your highest levels of consciousness, and you have enough time, as you are already aware, to accomplish in this lifetime what you yearn to accomplish, and whether you wish to do it all at once or spread it over various times and places is entirely up to you and your Soul's wisdom and your Soul's design.

< 122 >

DIALOGUE EIGHTEEN

22 March 1982

E: Are you aware, my friend, that instead of being positioned on your left and my channel's right, as I have been in our past communications, I am on your right today, as I usually am in your times of meditation? I do this for a double reason. One is to allow you to assume the posture of the receiver in a familiar way so that we can enhance our individual communication together, you and I, which has already begun as a most valuable process, and also to unstick, if you will, a little the Consciousness of my dear companion so that she can truly begin to relinquish what has seemed to be a very comfortable but also limiting aspect of her life. Freedom, my dears, freedom, to allow, to be, to breathe in and to exhale the reality of God, the reality of Spirit, the reality of your own eternal Beings.

And now I would well like to admonish and also to celebrate. The reason for celebration is that you are being allowed, by the request of your highest wisdom, of course, to enter into a new and quite different realm of learning and experiencing. Did you ever consider

< 123 >

photographing the Spirit, that is, photographing the Life Force that is the true Reality?

W: Not really, Emmanuel. I've always shied away from what I used to call "psychic whoopee."

E: There certainly was a time when it was very misused, very maligned, indeed hokey.

W: I'm surprised to hear that word *hokey* coming from you, Emmanuel, of all people.

E: Some of the new phrases are indeed quite remarkable, are they not? And yet is it not time, as we expand and explore the various means by which the reality of God can be made known to those who exist in the physical earth, is it not time perhaps to reconsider your original condemnation and to open your gifts and your expertise to the service of the Spirit? Consider it. This is not a mandate, it is a suggestion.

W: But what about my work with people who have cancer, then?

E: This will enter exactly into the mainstream of what you are beginning to do with those who are involved in the experience of cancer, which is limitless in its potential and brilliant in its capacity and is truly God's work, but what I am speaking of now is not a substitution but an addition. By being able to show that all things on earth possess a light, a glow, in other words a Consciousness that goes beyond the human and enters into the Divine, there will be the opportunity to expose the

< 124 >

cancerous experience as not something that is contr
to the human well-being or to the Laws of Nature, but
something that has been requested and willed by one's
Higher Self, even created by It.

Nothing exists in your human world, my dear friend,
that does not also exist in the world beyond, and
therefore all things are of God, even the cancer cell,
although this is difficult to conceive of when one is
experiencing such an attack, such a learning process.
And yet you and I know that this is true, and through
the developing and honing of the photographic mode
that I am suggesting, and with our assistance, of course,
one will be able to experience and to see the Life Force
flowing in all things and thus have a better acquaint-
anceship with the deeper meaning and the deeper
reality of a misfiring cell. And indeed, one may say
quite simply that a cancer cell is saying "No" instead of
"Yes." But it has a Consciousness, and even though it is
saying "No," it can be taught to say "Yes" again. All
cells in the body are initially in complete agreement
with the Divine Consciousness, but when the consciousness of the human being begins to defer, begins
to acknowledge other masters, other wisdoms above
this innate knowing—and I speak on all levels now, you
understand that, all levels, conscious, subconscious,
physical, mental, emotional, as well as spiritual—then
the body must eventually react to this in order for the
human being in its humanness to be made aware that it
is in some way defying its own Divinity. And so a
cancer cell is not a bad cell but a cell that is answering
and reacting to a negativity within the human being and
is even in its cancerous state serving the Consciousness
of the Soul.

< 125 >

And I will tell you something, my friend, when you are able to show on an energy-spiritual level the benign nature of the cancer cell then the ignorance and the fear will be erased and it can be taught to say "Yes" again.

W: As usual, Emmanuel, you're way ahead of me. You're planting seeds again.

E: Yes, my dear Wingate, I am, but as you know painfully from your own life as well as from those whom you are now touching with your wisdom and love and truth, there is a great denial of light in your world of Light. A painful thing, certainly, and one that we have vowed and committed ourselves to rectify, and as our growing, our working together, continues to evolve, we will to a more and more conscious degree be able to share and to exchange, and in that sharing and exchanging all that I require of you is that you be open to what is being suggested, but if there is such a gradation of Consciousness, of Energy in your human physical world that the awareness and Spirit cannot function as we would like, why then we will find another way.

W: You know, Emmanuel, this couldn't be happening at a better time. When I first imagined what I look like as a Soul way back when I was at the apex of my cancer experience, I saw myself as an old shepherd with long gray hair sitting on a rock and holding a shepherd's crook in my right hand, but not too long ago the image began getting younger and younger, until now it's of a vibrant, vigorous young man ready to begin a whole new cycle of experiencing.

< 126 >

E: The vision that the Soul brought in of a wise and contemplative and noninvolved old shepherd needed to be altered, for what is required now is not only wisdom of the contemplative types but wisdom physically manifested.

W: It's as though I've gotten my second wind, Emmanuel.

E: Exactly, and the revitalization of your body through the process you chose to deal with your cancer has allowed for this to happen, but you do not have to gear yourself up for another time of such painful growth. This cycle will be much more benign than the last one. Indeed, the image that you have held of yourself as being rather contemplative and noninvolved is already being transformed into that of a man of experiential reality, and as this becomes more and more a part of your human consciousness then what I have suggested originally in this communication will not seem so strange.

W: I do see myself getting more involved in the world.

E: And allowing yourself to put aside the mantle that you felt you were required to place upon yourself and let some of that old excitement back in. It will not undermine what you have to offer or what you and I are building together. It will invigorate it. It is indeed a time of revitalization and rejuvenation, and when I speak of revitalization and rejuvenation I am speaking not only of the mind and the body but of the Life Force itself. I thank you for your love, my friend, and your faith in me

< 127 >

and our communication together. There is great deal that can be done through this, not only for your growth, which is, of course, of paramount concern and interest to all of us, but also for the work that we will be doing together.

Let me begin to consider how we can alter the present state of relative unawareness, but first I would like to challenge that in its overall concept. You are indeed aware that we exist in a mutuality, and you are, and I lovingly insist that you claim this for yourself, aware that I am often beside you. Now you may not perceive me in a particular way. Do not demand that, but allow simply for the knowing to be a proof of the perception. That will stretch you in your seeking of faith and honesty. Indeed, there is a great deal to be learned simply from saying "I may not consciously know it now, but I know it." What strength will come from that I cannot begin to tell you. And then as you begin to experience this new phase, as you question, as you reach, as your mind begins to circle from belief to disbelief, which can happen in a flash, as you know, where you say "But what do I do here, I don't know what to do here, I am not hearing what to do here, I do not understand this," that is when you must also begin to say habitually "My conscious mind may not under-stand this but my heart does and my Soul most certainly does, and so I will flow with it."

W: The holistic doctor I've been going to says that at least at the cell level I have the body of a twenty-five-year-old lumberjack, which means I've pretty well got-ten rid of a lot of old toxins in my body, and now I have

< 128 >

to finish the job by getting rid of a lot of old attitudes as well.

E: Exactly. You need to allow what you have so assiduously created, or re-created, to function.

W: I need to get off my rock and start taking care of my flock.

E: But remember, my dear friend, the young shepherd does not have to be sure of himself all the time. Enthusiasm and love and the vibration of true faith are enough.

W: Keep talking to me, Emmanuel, I need to hear things like that again and again.

E: I will, my friend, I will. And you are hearing me much more frequently, I'm sure you are aware of that.

W: Yes, dear Emmanuel, I am, but I wish it could be even more than it is. I guess I'm insatiable.

E: I realize how eager and willing the Spirit is within you, and it's all a matter of unlocking the last door. Indeed, it is unlocked, and it is simply a matter of allowing it to open. It will be like learning to walk all over again, like learning to speak and not being sure that the words will be understood or that you will pronounce them correctly. It doesn't matter, it simply doesn't matter. You are in a time of growth and you must trust. Be not only patient with yourself but be

< 129 >

charitable also, for you will not always know exactly. That is not necessary, do you hear me, my dear friend, that is not necessary, not for you. You can err on the side of inadequacy, of not knowing, of inexperience, but not on the side of denial. Not any longer.

There is a great deal of work to be done in the precious world we all love so dearly, in the wonderful schoolroom that has served so many so well. It is ailing, not terminally but ailing, and it requires love and support and identification with its higher meaning and its higher purpose.

Do not mourn the misuse that is heaped upon it, for those who come, come not only with fear and unknowing but also with a Soul that is deeply longing for Light and Truth. Welcome all into the schoolroom and do not judge, difficult as that may be, do not judge, but see all, each one, as a light seeking Light through the maze and jungle of their own darkness.

W: So it seems as though perhaps the most important thing that I have to offer those who come to me with cancer are the insights that came to me when I was going through it myself.

E: Absolutely, you could not do your work without it. But you are now, in a symbolic sense, coming to grips with the thieves in the temple. You cannot be passive or too benign when you are faced with a self-destructive attitude. That does not mean that you are the stern father, not at all, but it does mean that in your passivity, in your total acceptance of your oneness with God, there needs also to be a more active and challenging force.

< 130 >

W: Supposing, Emmanuel, that deep, deep down a voice tells me that someone doesn't really want to live.

E: You ask them if this is true. It would be a very courageous thing for you to do.

W: Would they really know, Emmanuel, or would the answer be so buried that they would feel that they were being completely honest with themselves when they said it wasn't?

E: Whether their conscious mind quickly runs to close the door or not, they have heard you, and though you may see horror and rejection and rage in their eyes, deep down they do know and their Soul is saying either "Yes" or "No."

W: If I felt that at the Soul level they really wanted to die, Emmanuel, shouldn't I still try to help them?

E: Now we are coming to a question of dynamics and definition. Help them what? Help them to find their own peace, help them to experience their decisions without pain? Of course.

W: Even if it would be to die?

E: You are there to help them, my dear friend, regardless of what their Soul's decision may be. Help does not always mean cure. Help means educate, and the beauty of an illness that brings one to crisis, as cancer does, is that it allows for a crash course in Spirituality, which, I might add, you graduated from very well.

< 131 >

W: Thanks so very much to you, Emmanuel.

E: Not at all, my dear friend, not at all. I only spoke to what you already knew and believed.

W: Once again to go from the sublime to the ridiculous, Emmanuel, you won't believe this, I hardly even believe it myself, but over the months my prostate, of all things, has become enlarged to the point where my plumbing system just isn't working very well and I'm faced with the strong possibility that it will shut down completely any time now, and that of course means an operation, and after five years of struggling successfully with cancer and not having surgery it seems that to have it now for such an almost frivolous reason would just be a bad, bad joke, and I wonder, Emmanuel, if there isn't some other way to deal with it.

E: My dear friend, let me take from you this troublesome detail and allow yourself to go about your business unscathed and unhampered. It's simply ridiculous to think that after all the supreme effort, all of the growth, all of the deep belief that you have earned and learned at this time, you would allow such a thing still to exist. This, my friend, is the admonition I promised you. What are you holding on to? Why do you feel that it is essential to deny this most important portion of your manhood? Have we not spoken of your body becoming younger? And can you not also offer this portion of your being to the rejuvenating process?

It simply does not follow suit, does it, that with all else becoming more revitalized, more energized, younger—yes, I would use that word, younger—that

< 132 >

you would hold on to such an archaic image of yourself as a man. So let's push this whole thing aside, that's all.

W: It's not just my prostate, Emmanuel. It's getting so I can't see, either. Those cataracts of mine are getting larger also, to the point where I'm stumbling over things and bumping into people and having problems driving, and I'm beginning to wonder if I shouldn't have surgery and get it over with before I hurt myself.

E: Not yet, my dear Wingate, give it another chance. A cataract, as you know from our past conversation, is simply a veil that one pulls across one's vision to avoid seeing the stark reality of what, for a great part of one's life, one has found unacceptable. But now that you are learning—by leaps and bounds, I might add—to accept what is there, even to the dread cancer that has become the favorite focus of negativity in your human community, now it is no longer necessary to have those curtains there, is it?

And now that you know that what you see is transformable, and you know this experientially and not just intellectually, and there is an important difference there, and now that you are beginning to move into a time in which you will be an instrument for such transformation in your work, then it is again no longer necessary to keep the shutters closed or the blinds down, and so let us allow for the very good possibility that, from this time on, this shielding will simply begin to dissolve and disintegrate, a little at a time.

The true reality is that you are safely surrounded by the eternal love of God. Let it soak through every pore in your body and let it heal you, let it revitalize you, let

< 133 >

it open your heart ever deeper and deeper to trust. To trust. The more that trust is evoked, the more that the decision to belong to God is expressed and believed, the more all things are Light and beautiful. But no operation, no surgery, not unless you really feel that is what you want to do.

W: I don't, Emmanuel, I really don't. You know how I feel about surgery.

I'm just sitting here thinking what harmony there is between you and me, Emmanuel. So much of the time your words could be my words. I guess sometimes they are.

E: Sometimes they are, my friend, sometimes they are. Should we speak to other issues? I think not.

< 134 >

DIALOGUE NINETEEN

17 April 1982

W: I know it's been only two weeks since I was last here, Emmanuel, but it's been a really rough time for me both physically and emotionally, especially emotionally, and I felt I just had to talk with you again, and now that I'm here I don't know where to start, but perhaps the physical part would be easier for me to talk about, so why don't I begin there.

It's my prostate again. The problem got worse instead of better, as I hoped it would, so I went ahead with the investigation I started and then discontinued after our last meeting and saw several doctors, each of whom had something different to say. One felt that it was not so much physical as emotional and that I just needed to relax. Another said there was a hardness in the prostate that he felt indicated malignancy, but that in any case my prostate was enlarged and should be operated on, and you know how I feel about that. And a third felt that the hardness would usually be an indication of malignancy, but also felt that surgery was probably unnecessary and gave me some medication to reduce the swelling. And so now for the first time in five and a

< 135 >

half years I've had at least one doctor tell me that my cancer has become a real and threatening problem again, and I can't help but feel concerned.

E: If one were to examine most closely the condition of your prostate at this time, dear Wingate, one would find a very small amassing of what could be judged to be troublesome tissue, and yet I cannot allow myself, or you, to be locked into a diagnosis of words. I don't care what you call it, it has no significance, and there is therefore no reason for the vocabulary that was used to be of concern to you.

W: Thank you for your gentle reassurance, Emmanuel, but I'm not nearly so concerned at this point about cancer or even whether I live or die as I am about what's happening to my deep and abiding trust in you, all because the last time I was here you said to let you take from me what you referred to as this troublesome detail and to go about my business unhampered and unscathed. And I really felt as though I released it to you, Emmanuel, and yet here I am more scathed and hampered than ever. It seems as though I spend half my life rushing to the bathroom and the other half not quite making it, and it's getting harder and harder to go about my business and I'm having a great crisis of faith.

E: My dear friend, in your willingness to yield to powers beyond the conscious mind you must be willing to lose what you hope to gain, to accept what you hope to relinquish. In other words, one does not surrender and still maintain demand. One surrenders in order to allow what is to transpire to transpire, and it is in the duality of

< 136 >

the deep inner conflict that the present circumstance still abides within you, though you were assured that this would depart, and it will indeed depart. There is no need for unconscionable concern, but only a readiness to allow for the will of the Soul to be done and the future to take care of itself. I relinquish nothing of my former statement. Only I must add a request that you give time and patience and willingness to what I have said. This is not an issue of forcing but of relinquishing, but if one relinquishes, one must relinquish all, even the expectation of or hope for what one most desires.

If I were to say to you, for example, that at the moment of surrender you would be instantly healed, it would defeat the purpose, would it not? And it is therefore a necessity for you to be willing, and quite truthfully willing, to surrender to whatever circumstance comes about in this situation. I can faithfully and safely tell you that this is not a life-threatening thing. But it is, in a manner of speaking, a new area or arena in which to practice what you have longed so to accomplish in this lifetime, which is the deepest and the profoundest, absolute, and unthinking trust. Often you have prayed to the area within you that still withholds its total acceptance. The doubt, the doubt, my friend. We have spoken of this many times, you and I together. Is this not an excellent opportunity, then, to relinquish doubt, regardless of what transpires in human form, and to choose rather to follow your budding surrender to its fullest bloom?

W: That is such a difficult concept, Emmanuel, I wonder if you would go over it again, in perhaps a slightly different way.

< 137 >

E: It will be my pleasure, of course. What I am saying as clearly as I am able from my Consciousness to yours is this, that the only requirement is that you relinquish all requirement. Even the need, the desire, the request, which is most understandable, to be completely healed must be relinquished. We are speaking now to matters of gossamer, of great subtlety, for one can very readily be willing to accede to the request or promise of another if in that yielding one is guaranteed what one wishes.

But you are now longing in the depths of your Soul to taste and to understand complete Surrender to the Will of God, and I as a servant of God am most willing to offer you this opportunity to practice a state of complete equanimity and total indifference as to whether you are healed in this way or not. In other words, so long as you cling to a particular image or demand as to what it is you hope will transpire, then you have failed to surrender totally—is this not so?

I am teaching you something very important here, and my intent is to usher into your Consciousness the most difficult concept of all, that of complete and total Surrender. This is the real purpose of your present discomfort, and it holds a great and deep value for the growth of your Soul. Therefore, at your request, and on the advisement of the Spirits of higher intent, I offer you this blazing and loving alternative, which is to relinquish completely all demand and all need or desire to bring about a desired result as you foresee it and instead to yield, to give over, to Surrender to the totally unknown.

In all of your lives in which you have striven for excellence, for victory, you have been successful; often

< 138 >

you forget that. There has never been a time that what your Soul reached for it did not accomplish, and yet this is both good and bad. It can have a most positive effect on the sense of self-worth, and the feeling of being able to cope and to function in the physical world, and this has been of extreme importance in bringing you to your present state of awareness.

But then there comes the moment when all the rules seem to be turned upside down, when you seem to enter, as it were, into another realm of existence, where what brought you there is not only a necessity but even a deterrent, and you have come to that point. Your determination has been a wonderful attribute. The learning, the processing that you are experiencing are all invaluable. I wouldn't change one iota of it.

But now this new element has come into your life, and what a blessed time it is. All of us who love you and cherish you on this side of Consciousness are most grateful for it, though we are aware also of the struggle that you are now experiencing. To surrender to the Unknown is most difficult, to hand over the tiller to someone else has always been for you a task of magnitude, and so to relinquish without foreknowledge of not only the how or the when but also the if, this must seem to you to be the most difficult of challenges. And yet, dear Wingate, you must ultimately learn to depend not on your own will but on a Higher Will and the Forces that bring you and connect you to the Will of God.

W: So then the whole point of this ridiculous problem of mine is actually a golden opportunity for me to learn total Surrender.

< 139 >

E: Exactly. You have come to the final challenge in the Soul's evolution, dear Wingate, and it is without question the most difficult task of all.

W: How humiliating that my final challenge has to do with something so almost frivolous.

E: But so fitting, dear Wingate. In the sense of grandeur that so pleases so many, including you and me, I am sure it would be far more satisfying to be confronted by a den of lions, and yet how humble, how sweet to allow yourself to join humanity in its deepest humanness in order to join Spirit in Its most lofty wisdom and Light.

We will walk this humiliating path together, dear friend, and do not for one minute doubt that I have not walked a similar path myself. I have, and I thought at the time that it was the deepest human degradation, whereas I found it was really the shortest road to Light. But it *is* a devil of a problem, isn't it?

W: You know it is, Emmanuel, especially since I'm not supposed to do anything about it. And yet I'm sure that sooner or later a little voice is going to tell me to be practical and have other things lined up, like doctors, just in case.

E: That's all right. Be as practical as you feel you need to be.

W: So here I would be on the one hand surrendering to the Will of God, the Unfolding Plan, not knowing what they are, and on the other hand most willfully

< 140 >

planning my strategy just in case things don't go the way I would like them to. That seems like a complete contradiction.

E: Not at all, my friend, not at all. You became human in order to give substance and breath to Spirit, and in order to sustain your humanness as you go through your Spiritual tasks you may at times honor the humanness if the humanness is not up to the task of the Spirit. And so don't in any way condemn yourself or put limits on what you do physically while you are in the process of learning Surrender.

W: In other words, I should take the medication I've been given.

E: If you feel that you need it, knowing that while you are honoring the physical you are in no way dishonoring the Spirit.

W: But wouldn't it be showing a lack of trust in you, Emmanuel?

E: If you truly do experience a lack of trust then that is what it is illuminating, but if you are merely showing kindness to a portion of you that is not yet capable of total Surrender then this is to be respected. Don't you see, my friend, you live in two Realities and at times it is very difficult to bring them together. Indeed, it is often not necessary, for once you have gotten beyond the point of identification with the physical, though it is a schoolroom, though it is your text, and though it is a most valuable means of learning, it is no longer who

< 141 >

you really are. You know yourself much more deeply than that.

So should you long to Surrender, trusting that whatever happens is the Divine Will and that it is for your ultimate good, and should you find your body making your human experience untenable or uncomfortable, then it would be quite foolish for you not to take steps to have your physical body functioning again. And to alleviate your concern, and once more acknowledging the difficulty of conceptualization in words, you are Spirit, my dear friend, and what the Spirit is conscious of, what you in your humanness are longing for, these things will not be destroyed or contaminated if your physical body is no longer able to accede at this point to the demands of the Will or the desire of the Soul.

W: And yet this troublesome detail is such a good way to learn total Surrender, Emmanuel, much better than cancer, I'm so constantly aware of it.

E: But, my friend, you deal so literally with yourself. There is no question that you will ultimately learn Surrender, that goes without saying, but perhaps you demand of yourself something that you are not yet capable of doing. If this is the case then to allow yourself to suffer would be a cruelty that will most certainly get you not one step closer to total Surrender and Light.

W: Well, I'm not ready to give up on it yet. It would be nice, though, if just the most awkward part of my problem could be taken from me. At least with cancer I could go about my business, but this really gets in the way.

< 142 >

E: I know, this minor detail is something else, isn't it. It's really troublesome, but so much less important, dear friend, so much less serious.

W: And it can teach me such a precious lesson. I suppose I should be grateful for it.

E: Indeed you should, dear Wingate, for it is not only your teacher, but a blessed friend that is holding out another precious gift to you.

< 143 >

17 August 1982

E: I would very much like to commend you, dear Wingate, for the great effort you have been making to reach out to our union.

W: And there are times when I really feel it, Emmanuel, the Oneness, I mean, especially during my morning meditation, which I always start by affirming that I am a Soul, a Mind, a Consciousness, a body of glowing, incandescent Light, and that I am joined with you in the most deeply intimate communion. It's just that it never seems to last long enough.

E: I know, I know, but these things take time, so do not torture yourself or put yourself upon the rack, as you tend to do, and as your budding awareness of my daily presence in your life continues to grow you will find the experience becoming more constant.

However, the art of disconnection is far more highly developed in you dear humans than is the art of connection, not only with those of us in the Spirit world but, as you will readily agree, with other human beings

< 144 >

as well. It is a protective device that has become overdeveloped, as it were, and therefore the reaching out will become far more stressful, far more difficult, and requires far more effort than what now appears to you to be the negative ability to disconnect.

And yet there have been times when you were connected to the degree that you long to experience now, dear Wingate, though perhaps you did not recognize it as such at the time. There was bounty in your life, there was growth and peace within your Soul, and there was illumination in your Consciousness. And then there were those periods of withdrawal or doubt in which you entered again into the place of lesser awareness and lesser peace, but not so far, never so far as you had before. Indeed, the Consciousness is ever in a state of pulsation and fluctuation, for there is always the need for growth, there is always the need for expansion, and it cannot and must not be demanded that it remain fixed, even though the fixed point may be peace and comfort and Light.

So reach for my hand most certainly whenever the thought crosses your mind throughout the day, and know that I grasp yours in return, even though at times you may not be aware of it, for there are other times when you are. Trust those times, but also allow for the pulsation of your humanness, for the Consciousness to reach out and then to contract and then to reach out again. This is ever how it has been, and I cannot, even for you, my dear friend, alter that process. Indeed, if expansion were to take place at a considerably accelerated rate it would be extremely uncomfortable. There would be a disconnection with your humanness that would be agonizing. So allow for that, allow for the time

< 145 >

of coming back into your humanness, and as you accept that then the times of reaching out to the expanded Self will become more readily available to you. Are you with me so far?

W: Yes, dear Emmanuel, I'm very much with you.

E: The tendency, indeed, the proclivity to move away from Light, from fullness and joy and completion, is something that is inherent in the very molecular structure of each human being. After all, there is the belief that is woven into the very fabric of your human consciousness that once you are completed, once you have reached to the ultimate of your capacity to know and to experience in a given lifetime, then at that very moment the doors open and you are consumed. The superstition that if one is to grow then one must leave something behind is also woven into the human fabric, and in the language of humanity that constitutes death. Not perhaps in the total physical sense, but death nevertheless, and this is always in the human mind something to be avoided. Therefore, though you strive mightily to overcome this tendency and to accomplish in the expansion of your Being its fullest capacity, there is still the portion of you that whispers, that says "But this will mean the end of something, this will mean my finish, my death." And indeed, a portion of you will remain behind, or perhaps I should say be transformed as you move forward, and this to your human consciousness very much represents death. So be patient with yourself, dear friend, be patient. We speak often, you and I, and we will speak more often in the future. Simply allow for the times of silence, for the questioning

< 146 >

and the doubt and even the closing of the door. Do not belabor it, but simply allow it to be.

W: Why is it, Emmanuel, that even though I treasure those moments of our Oneness, when it comes to having a dialogue with you it feels better if there is a sense of separation between us with you either beside me or slightly in front of me?

E: It is very simple, dear Wingate. This is the normal conversational relationship, if you will, and it is more comfortable for you when the words are spoken at an arm's-length distance. However, when one can hold an inner dialogue, which is a most beautiful and imminent step for you, then our conversation will be not in words, but instead there will be a deep knowing of Truth that will require no separation between us.

And now, my dear Wingate, I would like you to imagine a castle, a Sanctuary, if you will, on top of some distant hill. Think of it as a space to go to, a place to be while you are still human. You are aware of how the Laws of Manifestation work, are you not, my friend?

W: Yes, Emmanuel. I even taught them at one time.

E: Of course. Then you understand my reason for asking you to envision this edifice, which, of course, is the first step in the act of its creation. Design it and furnish it as you desire, people it as you will. And do not in any way limit your dreams, your visions, your aspirations, dear Wingate, for they are most certainly an extremely important part of your power as a human being to create your own joy and fulfillment in this, the

< 147 >

most important of your human existences. So what will you have, what is it that you desire, and when you can be clear as to what would give you pleasure next, what would fulfill you most, put it forth forcibly for your vision to see.

W: But I already have a Sanctuary on top of a hill that fulfills all my needs, Emmanuel. It has a garden to walk in, with trees and rocks and ferns and moss and a pool that birds come to bathe in, and a special room filled with plants and stillness and light to meditate in, and it's right in the heart of New York, which is where we both agree I feel I'm needed most.

And besides, if I've come into this life with but one purpose and that is to learn total Surrender to the Will of God, then it seems to me that as a very integral part of that I should become a good partner and cooperate in manifesting that Will and Its Unfolding Plan in every way I can, which doesn't seem to leave any room for my own desires and aspirations, not anymore.

E: But the Unfolding Plan speaks to you as Desire.

W: I know it does, Emmanuel, but I feel that everything is telling me now to focus on Surrender, so I've put desire aside, at least for the moment, because I find it's just too confusing to handle them both simultaneously.

E: When you speak of Surrender it is quite clear, my dear friend, that you are longing to give yourself over to a Higher Will and to be filled with the unbelievable peace and joy inherent in such surrender. Therefore, I

< 148 >

would like to suggest that in order to reach your wished-for goal perhaps more quickly, you mark your path by visualizing specific physical steps or practices along the way. They can be in the form of a ceremony, but if they are, then allow for the ultimate purpose of the ceremony to dictate the ceremony itself.

One such practice might be for you to envision steppingstones around a circle in your room of prayer and meditation, where each stone brings you closer to the center and your special place of Surrender, where you can sit and allow yourself to open to whatever there is being given to you at that moment from the world of Spirit.

Another way for you to practice Surrender could be with Time. Whenever you find yourself being aware of the time, for example, whether the time be convenient or not, say to yourself, "Well, all right, that's what's happening now, so I will accept that now, at this very moment," and surrender to the reality of that time. Then flow with the time and do whatever you need to do to fulfill the purpose of the moment.

Things as simple as these will help to hold your focus on the point of Surrender and keep it from becoming formless, though ultimately of course it is. But you are not quite there yet in understanding, and therefore it is important for you to surrender through the imagination and through the structuring of various aspects of your life as I have suggested.

W: And I still have those vestiges, Emmanuel. After so many lifetimes of steering my own ship and getting pretty much where I wanted to go or what I wanted to have, it's not easy for me to let go of the tiller com-

< 149 >

pletely. But that's all I want to do now, so please don't
ask me how I want this Sanctuary furnished. I don't
want to manifest things for myself anymore. I know
how to do it, I know how to work the Laws of
Manifestation, but I want to use them to get not what I
want but what you and the rest of my Soul Family want.
What God wants.

E: I understand, my dear friend, but I would like to
address, if I may, the slight misunderstanding that in
your prowess as a creator of bounty in your human life
you have somehow completely disregarded your own
Divinity and have instead attributed your material success to the abilities of a very limited portion of your
Being. In other words, as you seek to know more and
more of God's Plan and the universal need for you to
create in certain specific ways, it would be well not to
set aside so completely your own abilities and your own
needs and desires as the man.

For all things walk hand in hand, hand in glove, and
if you can envision the hand as the human being you
know yourself to be and the glove surrounding it as
Divine Will, this might help you to surrender not only
to an outer Will but to your own will as well, and to
trust it just a little bit more.

And though you have manifested most beautifully in
your physical world the outer trappings that bespeak
your inner peace and joy, there is the doubt, the
questioning as to whether or not you have worked in
cooperation with the Higher Will. Don't you see, my
dear friend, that as you open to Divine Guidance it
permeates every aspect of your life, until there comes a

< 150 >

point that you dearly long for, where nothing you do, nothing you think, nothing you experience is separate from the willingness within you to glorify and to serve the greater Plan. Would it comfort and please you to know that to a great extent this is already true in your life?

W: It most certainly would, Emmanuel. It does already.

E: And so to the question of furnishing the Sanctuary. Let me again suggest that you ask yourself what would aesthetically, spiritually, physically, and mentally please you, for why should you not be part of the pleasure, why should there be the supposition that the instrument must only be an instrument and not also be part of the joy? You may not yet be clear as to where it is or what exactly is to be done with it, or indeed when you will go to it—well, that's all right. Let that be as it is and remain where you are, practicing and developing the habit of Surrender until such time as it is requested of you to leave your present Sanctuary for another one. Indeed, you will request it of yourself, and you will go there willingly, without question.

W: In March you suggested that you and I would be involved in a new kind of photography that would be very important in my work with people who have cancer, but I've been moving slowly on this because other opportunities have been opening up that have required most of my available time. And besides, dear Emmanuel, I'm not sure just what this new photographic technique is supposed to accomplish.

< 151 >

E: It will accomplish several things, my dear Wingate. It will show the auric response to any discrepancies in the physical body—in other words, any areas that have refused or have not discovered how to assimilate the wisdom available to them and have therefore become dislodged from wisdom and fallen ill.

It will show those who are seeking to relieve such illness the broad-reaching effect of this inner denial, whether it be conscious or unconscious. It will show the need for attunement in order to synchronize the consciousness of the different bodies that must coexist while they are human. And it will point the way for the further development of new diagnostic techniques, as well as new ways for arresting and reversing such discrepancies.

Think of it this way, my friend. If there is visible proof that the energies of the physical body are in a state of disarray at a certain point and that they are therefore not flowing with the broader Consciousness of the Being, it would represent a great step forward, would it not? It would bring to the awareness of those involved in the healing side as well as on the patient side that there is a Soul and therefore a purpose to all things, and that if they would but seek in the illness its purpose rather than simply to alleviate the discomfort, they could thereby bring about a total cure. And if patients were able to surmise the purpose of their illness they could then make the decision whether to forgo fullness and health for the small comfort of the original blindness and illusion, or to be willing to put aside what has seemed to be a place of safety in the interest of growth and health.

In other words, the photographs that I envision will

< 152 >

show quite clearly where the dysfunction exists as well as its meaning, not only on the physical and psychological levels, which are deeply important, but on the Spiritual level as well. And remember, dear Wingate, you are a man of Spirit. You are here not only to diagnose and heal illness in this manner, but more importantly to bring the breath of eternal Truth and Light to your work with the Soul.

W: You know, Emmanuel, I'm beginning to see cancer and other life-threatening diseases, at least in the case of people who come to me, as being God's fishhook. There's such an openness to Spiritual growth at that time, there must be more to what I'm supposed to be doing than helping them with their physical problems.

E: Absolutely. They are not there to talk just about cancer, and cancer is not there just to make them ill.

W: I hope you've noticed that I haven't even mentioned what I usually refer to as my "problem," Emmanuel.

E: I am well aware of that, dear friend, well aware of that.

W: Only now I see it as a wonderful gift, a wonderful opportunity for me to learn total Surrender. And by experiencing it in this way I really felt I had reached that space you talked about where there would be a sense of complete equanimity and total indifference as to what ever might happen or how it happened. As a matter of fact, I was in no hurry to do anything about the

< 153 >

situation because it was such an ever-present reminder to me to surrender, surrender, surrender.

But in the back of my mind there was always the thought that someday things might shut down completely, and then of course there would be no alternative except to go to the hospital for surgery. Well, last night it just about happened, and I had to face up to the very unpleasant fact that there was still something in me that resisted surgery, and that really hurts, Emmanuel.

E: Dear Wingate, you have been such an exacting teacher to this most stubborn and unwilling-to-learn portion of yourself. It is wondrous to behold how you have led yourself deliberately through areas of high hope and despair, of frustration and belief, to what now seems to be rock-bottom reality. So here you are, and though you have manifested many extraordinary things in your life, there are clearly some things, yes, even your own physical body, over which you simply do not have total control. Let us sit for a moment in deep gratitude and celebration, for had this been otherwise there would have been the false belief that the mortality, which is indeed the imperfection of your humanness, had become perfection. And it can never be thus, for by the very manifestation of your humanness in physical form you have created the imperfection that you are now seeking to transform.

Hold to this deep belief, that whatever ultimately is the outcome of this, it is indeed correct, and rejoice in the ability to be able finally to reach that pinnacle of understanding where in absolute truth you are quite right, it really doesn't matter what happens or how it happens. The moment that that pinnacle is inhabited as

< 154 >

completely and fully as your dear imperfection allows, you will then find that it truly no longer matters whether you go for surgery or you do not. Now I cannot promise that at this time there will be a miraculous cure, because then surrender would become a trick, a means to an end, and this it must never, cannot be, for the moment something so positive and lighted becomes a tool it loses its Light, as you already know, and becomes manipulation. Therefore, go with your present Consciousness and allow for whatever emerges to emerge, and if the time comes when you feel the need for surgery, why then so be it. What difference can it possibly make? After all, it is only a part of the imperfection that you have so perfectly manifested.

W: But the thought of going into a hospital and having surgery still triggers this little childish panicky feeling in me, Emmanuel, so I wonder if you would just please hold me in your thoughts and in your heart and put your arm around me now and then.

E: Of course, dear friend. Consider it done.

W: Thank you, dear friend, and may I more and more show forth our Light and love and joy and purpose.

E: The willingness, the deep and profound commitment will light your way. God bless.

< 155 >

DIALOGUE TWENTY-ONE

11 October 1982

W: This probably sounds strange, Emmanuel, especially in the light of my present circumstances, but I feel
very strongly that my life is in the process of beginning
all over again on an entirely new level of understanding.

E: It is not strange at all, dear friend. In reality life
begins every moment of every day. Nor is there such a
thing as a permanent ending to life, as you know. Even
death is not that, but merely a time of transition, a
doorway into a new and greater Reality.

In the same way, one does not end a time of health
and enter into a time of illness; one blends one's
consciousness into varying stages and degrees of learning. The moment that the concept of learning takes hold
rather than the sense of fear and apprehension, then
there is a total change in the metabolism of the physical
body. Now whether this results in a release from this
body—which is not bad, it is not a terrible thing—or
whether it results in healing is dependent upon the
purpose of the Soul and what It has come to learn or to
experience or to demonstrate. Indeed, there should be a

< 156 >

clause in any healing process that allows the Soul the choice of leaving, that allows death to be an acceptable alternative rather than a defeat. If death were a defeat, then who would win in your world? No one. And one would be born with feet of clay only to drag them painfully through a lifetime of terror to ultimate defeat. What a distorted, fearful, horrible, painful image that presents, and yet how many still dwell in such a nightmarish reality. You, my friend, are blessed with the opportunity to alter such horrendous images for those who come to you as well as those who will come to you in the future. Glorify the human potential, the body and the Soul's ability to transform illness into health. Of course, you are an excellent example of that, and one would wonder if you did not celebrate it to the highest. And yet also speak in the interest of love and learning in celebration of the broader reality that truly does exist.

Who then would fear cancer or any other illness once they knew, as you know, that death is but a greater expansion of Self and a more beautiful place to be, once one has completed the Soul's task in Its physical domain. So when you can and where you can, speak to both issues. It will be most helpful, and will offer not a sense of fear but a sense of safety. For you, of course, Surrender was the key to this.

W: *Surrender* is such a beautiful word, Emmanuel.

E: Indeed it is, and yet for most so distorted by their own misconceptions that it becomes not the pleasure in the expanded reality that it truly is but a thing of deep distrust and fear. How unfortunate, and yet how often

< 157 >

the human intellect can take the most benign and glorious sense of God within and turn it into something distasteful, weak, and degrading, merely because there is such disparity between the true meaning and the intellectualized meaning of the word *Surrender*, and because of a deep superstition, warranted often by human experience, I will grant you, that if one yields one will be devoured. But you and I, dear Wingate, are aware of quite a different definition of "Surrender," and this should be a most valued part of your teaching.

W: Yes, it's not as though one were to wave a white flag and give up to a more powerful enemy. It's opening up to a beloved, with a joy in your heart and a deep desire to serve the Divine Will and Its Unfolding Plan. And the joy seems to me to be such an essential ingredient, Emmanuel. Perhaps that's why, as a way of enhancing the depth of my own Surrender, I've been imagining myself in a boat on the River of Life, opening to It and Its Unfolding Plan and at the same time flowing with It and cooperating with It, and at the same time happily singing "Row, Row, Row Your Boat" and going through the actual physical motions of rowing. But not too hard, just gently. And *down* the stream instead of struggling furiously up it, as I'm so used to doing.

E: Or dragging your anchor and looking anxiously over your shoulder. And yet there is a natural human curiosity, if no longer a concern, as to what the next step will be, what the next decision will entail, and so on. This adds spice to life, and hopefully it will never be diminished.

< 158 >

W: I wonder what would happen if I looked over my shoulder and saw a rock ahead of me, Emmanuel. I would still probably be tempted to steer around it.

E: Because the rock would create anxiety. But supposing you could say to yourself at that moment, "There's a rock. I wonder what God has in mind for me there"?

W: With an open heart and a sense of joyous anticipation. That's what Surrender is finally all about, isn't it?

E: Yes, but so often there is a grim face that goes with it instead. You surrender and you're nailed to a cross.

W: Like Jesus. The cross for Him was the ultimate rock, wasn't it?

E: But unfortunately there is no awareness of the flow or of the internal workings of the Consciousness that said with a great deal of excitement and love and anticipation, "Oh there it is, I wonder what God has in store for Me now." We see only His agony, and that is unfortunate. For though there was pain most certainly, the anticipation of being lifted, even at the moment of human doubt, was joyous.

W: It must have been something He needed to go through. Otherwise, how could you explain how this greatest of Masters, who raised the dead and walked on water and who so confounded the priests in the temple when He was but a boy, did not make the slightest effort to escape from the Garden of Gethsemane, even

< 159 >

though he knew well in advance that He was going to be betrayed and that soldiers were coming to arrest Him? Or not make the slightest effort to defend Himself when He was brought before Pontius Pilate? In other words, He didn't try to steer around the rock.

E: Yes, why turn aside when the task is almost finished?

W: It's beginning to look as though my two problems are rocks I'm not supposed to steer around either, Emmanuel. They've gotten even worse, to the point where they're getting in the way of my work and I just don't know how long I'm going to be able to hold out and not have to have surgery, which just doesn't seem to make any sense. And yet if it does have to happen it must be for a reason, there must be a purpose, there must be a teaching somewhere. It must be part of the Plan, part of what I'm supposed to experience. And yet you feel it's not time to give up or rather open up and go to surgery, which I would still like to avoid if at all possible.

E: I am well aware of this, dear friend, and I would like to point out that self-healing is available to you, as you have already demonstrated with your cancer, and I therefore suggest something that is not often done, at least in this way, but the potential is there, and that is that you begin to touch the areas of affliction gently and often, tracing circles around them with your fingers very lightly and with a great deal of compassion and love and devotion to your own worthiness as a man and a Teacher, as a servant of God. As you gently encircle

< 160 >

the problem areas, see within them the residue of your past transgressions, if you will, for lack of a better word, and encompass them ever more slowly into a diminishing area until they become pinpointed in your Consciousness as simply very small specks of blackness, and then find within your heart the wisdom to allow for these specks to remain as a reminder of your humanness. Now it does not matter if there is not an immediate response to these daily ministrations. This approach is perhaps not as melodramatic as some, but in the constant gentle circling and diminishing of the identified areas of wrongdoing, you will be graphically redesigning the structure of your own energy currents, and there is a great possibility that the vibrancy that truly exists within your human abode will now rush to the troubled areas and bring about an alleviation or a reversal of the symptoms and ultimately a healing. And so begin tracing these gentle circles with the greatest amount of love for your Self and for the structures of your physical being that you can experience, and envision the areas that you still hold yourself accountable for getting smaller and smaller and smaller.

Now I am not suggesting that one must achieve complete self-forgiveness. That is something most devoutly to be wished for, but it is not necessary to bring about the healing. And make no mistake, dear Wingate, there is nothing, there is no dysfunction in your human world that is not capable of being healed by the Consciousness of the Soul. Although it is difficult to accept this Truth when one is ill, for there is a tendency to feel that one should somehow know better or have done better, or that somewhere one has failed or not done what one was supposed to do. And so, although I can

< 161 >

speak of these things to you, dear friend, it would be a most difficult concept to share with those who come to you, for there will not perhaps be the growth necessary to alleviate or deal with the sense of wrongdoing or guilt that can come with being told that they could have done something and yet they quite obviously have not done it.

W: I'm not so sure I won't feel as though I've failed somehow if I have to someday check into a hospital for an operation though, dear Emmanuel. I'd probably feel as though I'd let us both down. And besides, I don't think of surgery as something I can get much nourishment out of.

E: Yet I tell you, my friend, if ultimately you do choose at some level to enter a hospital, it will not be a defeat. Indeed, I will put my money on you that you will receive and give great teachings, and we will be there with you.

W: I like the feeling of "we" being with me. It's a very comforting thought for me to hold on to, much like "We will walk this path together, my friend, and you will be victorious."

E: Let me take your hand for a moment, dear friend, the right hand, for that is the one that holds within it the power of revelation. Place it upon the forehead of those you seek to help, and at the same time place your left hand behind the head at the base of the cranial area. This is a method of thought transformation that can

< 162 >

quickly alter the Inner Consciousness of those who come to you. You need say nothing. Simply remain in that posture in a state of openness and prayer for as long as you feel is necessary and let us who abide with you offer over suggestions deep to the Soul in conflict. No words will pass, but this is not necessary. What is being done here is essentially Soul work at a very deep subconscious level, and this can very readily bring about the revelation or insight that is needed. This can happen instantaneously or at a later time during the day or even in the form of a dream, or, of course, not at all if the openness is not there.

W: There was a time when I would have found it very difficult to turn myself over to another will so completely, Emmanuel. But not anymore. I've already surrendered to the One Will, which has to be the only will there is, and It expresses Itself through thee and me, and of course everyone else if they could but realize it.

E: Exactly. Even those who perhaps are less evolved and less aware and who are to an incredible extent steeped in darkness are still, even at that level, expressing Divine Will.

W: I find that there is a lot of resistance when I say things like that.

E: And quite understandably so. It's confusing, yes. When one has accepted to some degree a dichotomous human world with both darkness and light, good and

< 163 >

evil, and so on and so forth, and one is then told that darkness also is following in its own way the One Will, there is bound to be resistance, for that seems to presuppose that darkness is not negative and that those who are destructive, harmful, vicious, and cruel are not that way at all. And though this is to a great extent true, it is a way of seeing that one can begin to experience only toward the close of one's reincarnational cycle.

W: There's so much I have to be thankful for, Emmanuel, so much I feel I have to offer now.

E: Which most certainly includes the blessing of your previous affliction.

W: That's a big part of what I have to offer, isn't it?

E: A very big part.

W: And it just so happens that I'm giving a cancer workshop tonight, and I plan to wind it up by talking about this blessing and suggesting that, even if things had gone the other way, which at times it seemed as though they might, it would still have been a blessing, although I'm glad it came out the way it did.

E: You were meant to remain in your human form in order to bring to others this message. Otherwise you would have been just as glad to leave your body.

W: And be with you at last without that glass between us. What a wonderful thing that is for me to look forward to.

< 164 >

E: And I as well look forward to it. But not yet. You still have work to do.

W: Yes, perhaps my best work, my most important work.

E: It is yet to come, truly it is yet to come.

< 165 >

DIALOGUE TWENTY-TWO

2 February 1983

E: Despite your growing willingness to love your humanness, my dear Wingate, and there has indeed been a great deal of success in this area, there are still times when you feel that the human part of you is perhaps an anathema to the spiritual strengths that you are developing more and more each day. Hold your humanness gently, my dear friend, gently. It has come a long way. It has done a great deal of magnificent work. It is to be trusted, not held suspect, for even in its incapacities and blindnesses it can be a valuable piece of machinery until it is finally put to rest.

Being human is no more a humiliation than being anything else, although you dear Beings of Light who are seeking to follow the Will of God find it very awkward and unpleasant to stumble over. If it can be seen not as a stumbling but as a joyous meeting, a reunion, perhaps, of pieces of you that you had forgotten existed, like an album of old photographs, something to be recognized with love, something to be enjoyed, then your process of transformation will hurry along quite rapidly.

< 166 >

W: I'm afraid there are two or three pictures in that album that I have trouble opening my heart to, Emmanuel.

E: I know, dear friend, but, and this may seem like a stern text to you, the Schoolroom of Imperfection is to teach love, not the reaching for perfection. If one can learn to love in an essentially unloving world, one has come a long way, wouldn't you say? And it all, of course, must begin and end with one's inner feelings about oneself.

W: And my favorite commandment tells me what those feelings should be, but I'm afraid I wasn't able to love myself enough, or it was the Unfolding Plan, or perhaps a combination of both. In any case, I finally reached the rock of surgery that had been looming ahead of me for some time now and the current that I had hoped would safely carry me around it piled me up on it with a resounding crash instead.

First, in mid-December my eye doctor said that the lens in my right eye, the one I could hardly see out of anyway, had gotten paper thin and must be taken out before it started leaking a toxic fluid, and so I had to go into the hospital and have that taken care of. And at the same time my prostate situation reached the point where it was getting much too much in the way of my work and what I felt I should be doing, so I went back into the hospital after Christmas to have that taken care of also.

And you know, Emmanuel, although I had surrendered to the idea of surgery months ago, years ago, I found there was a big, big difference between surren-

< 167 >

dering to the idea of it and surrendering to the reality of the surgery itself. But I fasted and meditated a lot before the first operation, and was calm and open and even curious during the actual surgery, which was done with a local anesthetic. I even fell asleep at one point when things got a little dull.

After such a (for me) great victory I could hardly wait to test myself and the depth of my surrender with the much more serious and difficult-to-deal-with prostate operation. But I prepared for it in the same way, and found to my great joy that I was just as open and surrendered as before. As a matter of fact, the last thing I remember before the anesthesia hit me was laughing uproariously with the surgeon and his whole supporting cast. I know you once said that if I ever did have surgery it would be a great teaching for me, and for the doctors and nurses as well, and you were so right, it turned out to be all of that. At least the feedback I got later seemed to confirm that it had been a very special experience for them.

And it was certainly an incredible experience for me. As a matter of fact, I was able to surrender so deeply that I really felt that's it, that I had done it, that I had surrendered totally. But you know, Emmanuel, it wasn't more than a few days before something told me that there was still more surrendering to do, and that something turned out to be right.

Sure my prostate wasn't working too well, which isn't at all unusual after surgery, and my vision wasn't all that great either, which is also not unusual after surgery, but I had no problem surrendering to either of those. Nor was being told I still had cancer a problem. You and

< 168 >

I both knew that anyway. But when I was being fitted with a contact lens the doctor noticed something that suggested I might have a brain tumor, so he rushed me off for a CAT scan, which showed that I did indeed have one, sitting right on top of my pituitary gland. And that *was* a problem.

Here I was thinking I had finally taken care of all my physical problems, at least all the important ones, and in the process learned total Surrender, and instead I had a brain tumor that had been around for no one could tell how long, but that could be growing very rapidly, in which case I probably wouldn't be around for very much longer. So, although I had become friendly with death because of my cancer, it looked as though I had better learn to really embrace it now, which, to my great surprise, wasn't nearly as difficult as I thought it would be. I had been given another gift, Emmanuel, perhaps the biggest gift of all, and this time I felt I had really done it, I had really learned my biggest lesson. At last I was able to surrender all my expectations, and as soon as it happened all my anxieties about the Unfolding Plan and what might happen to me completely disappeared. I've never felt so joyous, Emmanuel, or so free. It's been just an incredible experience, and when the time comes I'll be ready, but meanwhile I'm very happy right here, right now.

E: And that is a great accomplishment indeed. I'm so proud of you, Wingate. You came into this life to learn Surrender, and you by God have learned Surrender.

W: By God.

< 169 >

E: I knew you could do it. I knew when the chips were down, when the final cards were dealt, if you will, that you would come up with a winning hand, and you have. And I quite suspect that the tumor will find its own natural way of dissipation. Indeed, I cannot see any need to allow it to linger, unless you really feel inclined toward that being the means for your making a hasty exit.

W: No no, Emmanuel, that's not the way I feel at all. It's been a great blessing, a great teaching, like every-thing else that's happened to me only more so, but it looks as though it has served its purpose, and, as you said at our last meeting, I have work to do, our work to do, and only when that's finished, whether it takes two years or twenty-two years, will it be time for death and our long-awaited reunion in the world of Spirit. In the meantime, all I want is to be a good partner, so in my meditation I've asked how I can best do that, and the guidance I've received has been first to ensure the continuation of the Communion of Souls and the church that is such an important part of Its outreach, and second to put some of the joy I now feel into *Tilling the Soul,* and also to soften the commitment I have sug-gested in order to make it more readily acceptable.

E: Exactly, for after all, dear Wingate, you are here not just to speak to the few who are already indoctrinated, but to woo the many who are seeking as well.

W: I've already started on both these projects, Em-manuel, and they're going extremely well and I feel that

< 170 >

I'm making great progress. And then remember how last August I spoke of my deepening awareness of you and the rest of my—our—Soul Family, and how I felt that we were blending and merging and becoming one? Well, I feel this much more deeply now, to the point where at times there is no more "me" anymore but only "we," but then the "we" becomes "me" again, only now it's a much larger and more expanded "me" than before. It's as though I'm way out to here, Emmanuel, and it's very exciting because for a long time now, as you know, I've felt that this was the way the next step in my growth would be, that beyond a certain point I could become more conscious only by coming one with other Souls, and that this blending and merging I've been experiencing would go on and on and on until finally I and everyone and everything, separately and together, would become the One Soul, and that all this would somehow happen without there being any loss of I Am.

E: Exactly. As I sit before you now I am all that you are and all that you can conceive of being so long as you are still physical, but as one moves into the next living experience, which of course will be free of physical limitation, and you are already expanding to that point, one finds that there is a Consciousness that allows for total Oneness and at the same time Individuation. In other words, one's expanding Consciousness does not erase the Individuality of others, It encompasses it. And this does not in any way deny those Souls with whom one reunites their own sense of Individuality, it simply creates a Oneness within which the reuniting can take place.

< 171 >

Indeed, there has always been confusion as to whether one greets individuals in the next life or whether one experiences them as part of one's Self, and of course the reality is both. We continue to exist in our Individuality, yes, even to that ultimate moment of total and quiet blending with God. Now be patient with me, dear friend, it is extremely difficult and often impossible for me to create in your human language something that is beyond the limitations of that language.

W: I know, dear Emmanuel, but I found that I was able to hear you in that special place where there is no longer need for language or intellectual understanding because there is only one of us and our communication is not through words so much as just by knowing.

E: By being.

W: Yes, by being, like an Indian powwow where everyone sits in a circle smoking their pipes and then, as though at a signal, they get up and leave without having spoken a word and yet knowing exactly what had been discussed and what had been decided.

E: Exactly, exactly, for in Beingness all things are One, and as we merge there is that wonderful knowing that goes beyond vocabulary, and fortunately there is much beyond vocabulary, for, as you are finding more and more in your work, vocabulary can be exciting and illuminating but also limiting as well, and so we bypass vocabulary, you and I.

W: Except that hearing your words is at times very reassuring, dear Emmanuel. They reinforce my faith

< 172 >

and my trust and my still-developing sense of knowing.

E: Yes, I understand that, dear Wingate, but it isn't my words that give you the knowing, it is the knowing that allows you to understand my words.

W: However it works, I found that what you said touched me deeply, Emmanuel, and not just because it confirmed my own intuitive sense of what the next step and the next step and on and on into the infinite future is going to be, but it was also deeply moving for me to think how everyone has their own Emmanuel and their own Soul Family to look forward to becoming aware of, and then blending and merging and becoming One with.

But there's something about Oneness that caught me by surprise, Emmanuel. There's no more you anymore, no more wonderful you to hold hands with and talk with and walk with and just generally be with. There's only me, and I'm not sure I'm ready for that yet, at least not all the time.

E: I know, I know, and this is why I keep instructing you dear Souls to love your Selves, for then you will find that being with your Self is quite enough, yes, even to that moment when the Self will be all things and we will be home together.

W: It's certainly a lot easier to love my Self now that you and the other members of our Soul Family are part of It. But it's still important for me to experience you in your old familiar place here on my right, although it

< 173 >

puzzles me how I can be one with you and yet also separate from you.

E: It is simply that a part of you has moved from the Consciousness of Time and Space while another part of you still rests within that Consciousness, and so you experience me as both One with you and separate from you, and neither one is false. So for now let me sit next to you and also be One with you, and there is no contradiction here, only a difference in perspective. It is all One, dear Wingate, it is all One. Recognize the power that is now within you and get to know that Divine Being that you truly are, for only then can our work be truly done.

W: More and more I find myself saying things that are not at all what I would have said a few years ago or even a few months ago, and you know where I feel they're coming from, Emmanuel?

E: From both of us.

W: Yes, from both of us. How blessed I am to have you as my friend and Teacher, Emmanuel, my dearest friend and Teacher. My life just wouldn't be the same without you.

E: Glory hard won is glory never forgotten. You have earned every bit of your peace and your joy and your exuberance and your success, and now you have come to the dessert of your life's repast. Enjoy it, my very dear friend, enjoy it.

< 174 >

Afterword

The February 1983 dialogue turned out to be the final session Wingate had in Westport. Emmanuel's channel had stopped doing private sessions, and Wingate was now challenged to deepen his inner connection with Emmanuel, as he had been encouraged to do during their six-year relationship.

I had just resumed working with him when the final dialogue took place. I was stunned by the disclosure of his two operations and his brain tumor. He was oddly calm and at peace with himself, going about his daily tasks I would say almost jubilantly. By the time I would arrive for our morning meetings, he had had his daily communion with Emmanuel, written for two hours, and eaten breakfast. He would greet me with a hearty hug and smile, brimming with excitement for the work we would do.

—ALLAN RICHARDS

In May of 1987, following several months of weakening physical condition, Wingate made what he and Emmanuel talked about as being the final surrender, and peacefully and gently passed away. For those of us who knew him personally, he remains an immense source of strength and wisdom; and for those who have come to know him through his words, may he be an inspiration that Truth is within all of us, waiting only to be asked to reveal Itself.

—JOHN WINGATE, JR.